Depression:

My Witness, Your Solution

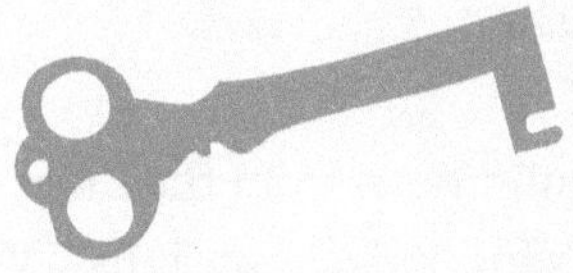

*Five easy steps to reprogramme
your little, inner monologue
and set your mind free*

Stelios Nicolaou

Dedicated:

To Chrystalla Theodorou Nicolaou, who has never failed to reveal to others and me what 'agape' love is truly about—a living sacrifice.

CONTENTS

Special Thanks and Acknowledgements:

–To Mrs Chrissie Flint who helped me with editing and publishing this book.

– To my friend Petros Georgiou, who cared enough to motivate me to keep on writing and to finish this book.

– To the personnel and managers of Sigma Café for all their help.

–To Yanni Chrisommalli, whose wonderful, progressive music introduced me to the beautiful world of simplicity, which can be applied in every area of our lives–including the development of the method of this little, book.

–Last but not least, to God, my heavenly Father and Creator, who has worked in the background, making this book possible.

What this little book
will do for you

The aim of this small book is to teach you how to develop a new thinking pattern that will replace the inner thinking that causes depressive thoughts and negative mood.

I believe simplicity is indeed *the ultimate sophistication*. That is why I have made every effort to keep complex scientific theories out of the range of this book. In fact some of these complex theories, I believe, I have managed to condense into simple principles, and a simple formula everybody can practice and master to defeat negative reasoning that leads to depression.

We will work together in a systematic fashion to teach you how to amuse and set aside negative thoughts that cause depression and bad moods.

Try reading the principles and do the simple exercises of the book. Reading, conceptualizing and rereading the simple steps of this method for thirty days, will help you internalize the principles and concepts of this book deep into your subconscious mind. Meditate thoughtfully on them for a while. Slowly, the new method, its concepts, and principles will become part of you. Do not worry about having difficulty knowing when to apply the new method. Pressure and life's little trials and challenges will do it for you. Just concentrate on learning and absorbing the principles and the steps of this new method. Pressure and difficulty are usually the best teachers.

It is a personal letter from me to you to tell you that things can improve. If things have improved for many others, I do not see why they cannot improve for you as well. It is my prayer that you will read this book, learn the principles, and apply this simple method. It is also my wish that this book will change your little, inner dialogue–defeating depressive thoughts.

I wish and pray for you to *complete the book with a new perspective*, a new attitude, and a new way of thinking, so a brand-new world will be revealed to you. . . .

May this book be the beginning to start viewing the world through different eyes and perceptions. May the ideas in this little book form the beginning of a new life–your life.

The author

CHAPTER 1

Our little, Inner Monologue

What is it?

What is our "Inner Speech," our "inner monologue?" Our inner speech or dialogue is how we converse with ourselves. It is the small voice in our head that we talk with–the mental process of the moment–that connects us with our environment. Your little, inner monologue is your communication bridge linking your conscious and subconscious mind. It is the way we form impressions about things; it is how we interpret external events related to our lives, our circumstances, and our environment–the inner monologue is the way we try to make sense of what is happening around us.

> *"It is very obvious that we are not influenced by facts but by our interpretation of the facts."* [1]
> Alfred Adler.

How important is our little, inner monologue?

As Alfred Adler states above, we tend to be influenced by the way we interpret facts than by the facts themselves. In a similar way, the ancient Greek philosopher Epictetus, said, *"Men are not worried by things, but by their ideas about things."* He also emphasizes, *"When we meet difficulties, become anxious or troubled, let us not blame others, but rather ourselves, that is: our idea about things."*[2]

Validating the ancient wisdom of Epictetus, a person's inner monologue has been shown in *research*[3] by medical and communication professionals, to have tremendous psychological and physiological effects on the health of the individual. In simple terms, our little, inner monologue may enslave us or may set us free. Indeed, *the way we talk back to ourselves* determines our emotional state: happy or sad; optimistic or pessimistic, friendly or hostile, depressed, or a free spirit.

Our inner monologue is our best friend who can easily become our enemy. With our self-talk, we may live in harmony, or be in a constant struggle, making our life "heaven on Earth" on one hand, or a "living hell" on the other. How much mental health and how much joy and fulfillment we experience in life is directly proportional to the quality of our inner dialogue, our little, inner speech, the way we converse with ourselves, by forming impressions about what is happening in life, in our circumstances, in our surroundings.

Another remarkable attribute of our inner self, as Epictetus pointed out is:
"our subconscious minds have no sense of humor, play no jokes and cannot tell the difference between reality and an imagined thought or image."[4]

> Our inner monologue *creates*, in other words, its own reality, which may or may not result in a *healthy mind*, or to a healthy understanding of reality.

Conclusively, taking into account the above ancient ideas coupled with modern research about the communication bridge between our conscious and subconscious, a main way of changing our subconscious programming is how we *reply to it*, through our little self-dialogue. We can change the impression of what is going on around us by the way we interpret events, or by the way we talk back to ourselves about what is happening to us–by improving, in other words, the quality of our little, inner self-talk.

A healthful inner monologue contributes to self-acceptance and self-love. A healthy self-dialogue confirms that we are in harmony with ourselves. It means that we accept ourselves as we are, and that we are at peace with the way we relate with our little, inner voice. It implies friendship and love with the "little voice-guy" that we are going to carry him around for the rest of our lives! In addition, when our inner monologue is harmonious, we are better in touch with our feelings, which means that we can enjoy and able to express the real part of us spontaneously.

When we are at peace with our selves, the communication bridge between the conscious and subconscious mind is harmonious. New information flows from the external environment and is easily communicated and assimilated in the subconscious mind. In turn, any relevant information is smoothly retrieved and examined from the subconscious mind to help with decisions at hand, while new information received from external stimuli is reshaping, perfecting our subconscious thinking.

The two-way channel is in harmony as the relation between the two components of the mind is harmonious as the conscious mind and the subconscious refreshes each other, building and strengthening each other as an ongoing process. A healthy outgrowing emotional and spiritual maturity is the result, as it is a product from our correct understanding of and a healthy relationship with, reality.

What is Depression?

The product of our inner talk is our *unique interpretation* of external environment and daily conduct. It is, in other words, the formation of our impressions about what is going on around us. Hand in hand with these impressions and interpretations we form from external circumstances, comes our emotional response as well.

A sensible conversation with our "little, inner voice" brings about harmonious, and positive emotional responses and conduct. On the other hand, a conflicting *interaction* with our inner self brings confusion to mind, causing an erratic behavior accompanied with negative feelings, stress, anxiety and of course many other symptoms of clinical depression. I strongly believe that the "chemical imbalance" medical definition of clinical depression is just a symptom of a distorted, unhealthy, inner dialogue in us. Depression, therefore, is mainly the product, or the "fruit" of our inner dialogue, the way we interact, talk, and relate with our inner little voice.

When this communication is distorted and altered by negativity, wrong beliefs and bad parenting, it is likely to lead to clinical depression, forming a vicious, never-ending cycle.

"Depression is ten times more common in people born after 1945 compared to those born before 1945."[5]

So, ten times as many people are becoming depressed *now* compared to fifty years ago (and this research takes into account increased reporting and public awareness). Human biology does not change that fast! Genes do not alter so rapidly–without the intervention of genetic engineering. Thyroid problems, food intolerances, allergies, and other physical illness can indeed lead to symptoms of clinical depression. Nevertheless, less than 10% of incidences of clinical depression are thought to have a chemical base. On the other hand, research suggests the amazing evidence that depression is not an inevitable result of difficult and adverse life circumstances. Only a percentage of people exposed to difficulties actually develop the symptoms of clinical depression.

Therefore, if depression is less likely to be the symptom of our genetic make up, and also if depression is less likely to be the result of dramatic, adverse circumstances as we go through life, clinical depression has to occur mainly by the way in which *we subjectively interpret* those adverse life circumstances and difficulties in our minds. To reiterate, if depression does not come from our "hardware,"–the way our body and mind are physically made, and if depression does not come from our life challenges themselves, then depression has to come from our software–our mind! I strongly believe that depression is the product of the way we think and reason, the way we evaluate, the way we crystallize impressions in our minds; the way we subjectively make conclusions about external events in our lives.

To make things more specific and clear, the cause of depression and negative moods are happening *because* of your inner dialogue between you and your "little voice" in your head. Depression is caused by of the way we think, the way we think about our thoughts, the way we evaluate our circumstances than the circumstances themselves–despite how adverse and dramatic they may appear. Our erroneous, subjective evaluation and perception, or the emotional label we attach to persons, events, and feelings in our lives is what makes us unhappy and depressed.

> Depression is caused by of the way we think, the way we think about our thoughts, the way we evaluate our circumstances than the circumstances themselves–despite how adverse and dramatic they may appear.

The Challenge. . . .

If the way of thinking is the root of depression, how do we simplify our inner monologue, or the thinking processes of the human brain, which is vaster and more complex than the stars and galaxies of cosmos, altogether? If positive thinking or talking positive to ourselves was the answer, we would have solved the problem of depressive thoughts a long time ago. Talking positively to ourselves has its merits; nonetheless, positive thinking alone does not seem to contribute to long-term maturity and emotional stability.

To analyze it a little bit more, the advocates of positive thinking claim that if we start talk positively to ourselves, we will be able to change almost everything. We can create reality from our own thoughts, they claim. Well, I do not think the law of gravity will change if we start thinking that such law does not exist, because we cannot create outside reality with our thoughts. The undeniable truth is that with 'positive thinking' we cannot change reality with our thoughts. Although optimistic thinking is preferable to pessimistic thinking, I have seen people who are quite optimistic and still live a life of misery. Life has its own rules and principles that positive thinking–no matter how attractive may be–does not seem to consider.

So here is the challenging question again: How do we change the inner monologue of the human brain? As the "little inner voice" inside is so stubborn and hurt, yet quite reactive, the little voice cannot be easily modified, corrected, or cheated, even if cheating implies a real and truthful new input. If our existing life script is difficult to change, how do we write new scripts, or reprogramme our thoughts since our thoughts are the root of depression? In addition, another interesting question would be whether it is realistically possible to rewrite our thought life once again?

The answer to the above challenging questions is that *change is possible* using a new perspective, a new way of viewing the world, a brand, new insight that you will gain–all packed within a simple method that will change your thought process, your inner monologue, your little self-talk, so that a *new world* will be revealed in front of your eyes.

In the chapter that follows, let us lay down the principles, foundations and structure, of this method, which will serve as *cornerstones* that will help you to apply the method *skillfully* in the daily circumstances in your life.

CHAPTER 2

Setting the Three Cornerstones for a Healthy Inner Monologue

You Just can't deceive your inner man, your inner monologue. . . .

In reality, we human beings have a natural tendency to feed ourselves with whatever values and principles we find it convenient to live by. "Everything in life is relative and subjective," we like to presume, and the modern, fast pace world we live in tries to do everything possible to shape us into this way of thinking. Somehow, we are convinced that we can confidently pick up what we want to believe, whatever "value system" suits us better–as long as such set of values is convenient and makes us feel good. "It's our life!" We exclaim in our attempt to assert total control of our lives.

"What upsets people is not things themselves
but their judgments about the things."[6]
From the Enchiridion, or Handbook of Epictetus

Validating the ancient wisdom of Epictetus, American author Robert Collier pointed out, *"our subconscious minds cannot tell the difference between reality and an imagined thought or image."[7]* In other words, our inner monologue builds its own reality of existence, its castle, its own little world–its subjective "virtual reality." Accordingly, we have become self-absorbed, approaching everyday problems *reactively* as we seldom have time to *question* our short-sighted view of life. As a result therefore, we tend to get busy with the individual trees instead of *zooming out* to view the forest and see where our life is heading.

We become so subjective, so biased and individualistic, with the resulting values to become *blurred* and *in conflict* with one other. Down deep, in the core of our humanity, nevertheless, our conscience is silently but persistently protesting.

This could not be more applicable in the case of today's modern way of living.   In this fast-moving, instant-gratification culture, people live like *isolated islands*, as we tend to make our own value system, our own set of relative principles, our own way of coping with life, and of course our subjective ways of finding a meaning in it. It is indeed a fact that modern life can condition us to be so egotistic, short-sighted and self-centered that we become so subjective, so biased and individualistic with the resulting values to become *blurred* and *in conflict* with one other. In reality, thus, we travel without a compass in a sea of ever-changing values. In the outer layer of our inner monologue everything we think and do may make perfect sense as we seem to use various rationalization techniques, so we can justify and classify everything as "normal" and acceptable–whatever decision we take. Down deep, in the core of our humanity, nevertheless, our conscience is silently but persistently protesting, "Probably something is wrong! Something is not right!" Our little, inner voice whispers, "It is not what I expected! It is not how I meant to live!"

The little inner voice in our conscience is crying out to us that our human identity is being undermined, our integrity diminished and disintegrated as we gradually lose our precious self-respect and human dignity. While on the surface all may look so rational, comfortable, and convenient, deep down we experience a gut feeling that *something is wrong,* that the way we are currently living does not make us truly happy–it is the realization that somehow we have not been true to ourselves for a very long time.

Thus, in our attempt to unclog our inner monologue from this turmoil, we need to establish the correct principles, or *the three cornerstones* for a healthy, functional self-talk. Just as any theory, machine, or system requires certain fundamentals to exist and operate, in the same way, your inner, little voice becomes functional and healthful when three, basic requirements and foundations are adequately established.

CHAPTER 3

First Cornerstone
for a Healthy 'Inner Monologue':
Rediscovering Truth

Our inner monologue has to operate with the cornerstone of *truth*. If it does not, strange things happen down deep in our human core. We just cannot cheat our "inner man"! Our private self already understands the difference between good and bad as it is part of our genetic make up to be able to discern–it is part of what makes us . . . human.

Sometimes we bury such notices with rationality, excuses, and other skilful games we engage. Regrettably, whatever attempts we make, the principle of garbage-in, garbage-out applies to our little, inner monologue, just as it applies in the case of a computer program. If you feed a computer program with false data, (garbage-in), it will give you wrong information and insights (garbage-out), however correct and flawless the calculations of the computer program might be. In the same way, our inner self will start at the end to protest in funny ways with not such positive effect in our self-talk and emotional well-being.

Many people may argue that *conscience* is the result of our Judeo-Christian values and all the value-related conditioning that we have received since we were children–that nothing is ingrained in our human nature. They argue that conscience is just a series of learned responses we have received, when we were children–nothing more. No mystery, no sacredness involved, no "DNA" conscience gene exists in the human spirit. What is right and wrong, they claim, is just part of our upbringing conditioning we received from our parents, schooling, culture, and society.

People from this school of thought also add that the mind can accept whatever values we feed into it–therefore, they claim, we can build the reality that perfectly suits our wants and needs.

Nevertheless, long before the Judeo-Christian values became popular in the Western culture, it is noticeable to mention that in mythology as well as in the everyday lives of ancient Greeks that the conception of "*Erinyes*[8]" existed. *Erinyes* were ghost-like, horrible-looking female creatures. Their job was to chase and punish people who did wrong. Fascinatingly enough, these terrible-looking, female ghosts could hardly cause physical harm to their human subjects. The main damage that Erinyes inflicted on their victims was spiritual and psychological. As a result, many of *Erinyes'* customers lost their sanity, losing their minds–not from the *Erinyes'* terrible-looking female-figures, but from the condemning thoughts *Erinyes* were able to whisper in their ears. Erinyes were in essence a conscience-control mechanism that generated thoughts of guilt, fear, and condemnation in people who were burdened by a guilty conscience. Simply said, *Erinyes* were targeting on what was already there–our *human conscience*, the primary, human component that distinguishes humanity from the animal kingdom.

What is Truth?
Does it exist–or is it just a creation of our minds?

The battle between Socrates and the Sophists[9]:

First we have to clarify that there is "absolute" truth. Living in a relativistic world, it might be difficult to admit and understand such a claim. Nevertheless, the battle between absolute truths over relative reality has been fought and won successfully more than two thousand years ago. It was the battle between Socrates and the Sophists.

The Sophists taught courses to the Athenians and other Greek cities 2,400 years ago that resemble so much our modern "quick success" schemes and "happiness now!" self-help courses and seminars, such as the following:

"How to win–no matter how unfair your case is."

"How to succeed in business without really trying, by using shortcuts that are not always honest and moral."

"The art of persuasion. How to persuade anybody for anything."

"How to succeed in life. How to play to win, no matter what."

Although the sophists' contribution to rhetoric, the art of persuasion, and logical thinking was substantial, in essence, the core beliefs of the sophists, if they had any, where:

1. Everything is relative–I can make my own value system, and I can still call it a truthful one.

2. While Socrates was questing for truth, searching for universal standards that govern the realm of human relations the same way physical laws govern the natural world, the sophists were claiming that no universal, objective standards, principles, or laws govern human existence. "Everything is subjected to our senses, in the way we perceive them," they argued.

3. The sophists believed that moral principles are not real, but merely the opinion of the individual or culture, as expressed in the famous line of the great sophist, Protagoras, who claimed, *"Man is the measure of all things."*

4. Some excerpts of some famous Greek sophists are:

> Protagoras, *"Man is the measure of all things."*
> Gorgias, *"Nothing exist."*
> Thrasymachus wrote, *"Might makes right."*

While Socrates searched for specific, eternal principles that were the glue of human relations and provided coherence and order to the human communities, the *Sophists*[10] were promoting ideas of relativity and subjectivity, where each person decides for himself what the true, the correct and the symmetric are.

The Sophists challenged, criticized and destroyed the foundations of traditions, the moral and social order, while they put nothing in its place—nor did they care. Many things in our world can be indeed subjective and relative though—however, objectivity as the foundation of truth continues to exist–despite our variable, ever-changing, emotional-based perceptions. In essence, the Sophists were saying that they could create reality with their mind, while Socrates refuted them and indirectly conveyed to them that they were liars, full of deception as they could not create reality with their limited minds. Reality, truth and objectivity exist outside the mind. The mind's *role* is merely to seek and understand the reality of those unseen laws that govern human existence, and to align our ways in agreement with such principles.

The Battle between Socrates and the Sophist continues today . . . .

This battle resembles in many ways today's way of thinking. "If it feels good, do it!" –as the popular slogan says! Although the question of the existence of absolute versus relativistic principles was answered 2,400 years ago, it is sad to end up 'downgrading' our brains and ourselves by adopting relativistic values and views that deteriorate our self-respect, dignity and honest principles that give genuine worth and meaning to humanity. Now in the 21st century, despite the huge technological advances since the time of Pericles, we have managed to reduce our human mind and live below the fundamentals–below what is obvious and true. By becoming 'neo-sophists,' we have created a false reality in our thinking with devastating consequences in our human spirit and inner monologue.

The battle between Socrates and the Sophists is the same battle we confront today, as it is the battle between universal, eternal principles that separate reality from illusion, and our shallow, subjective understanding of life. It is the battle of objectively derived reality versus the reliance on the ever-changing waves of our senses. It is the war between instant gratification versus delayed gratification. It is the battle between the cries of human conscience, and the hunger of man's emotional and physical needs for immediate gratification.

Aren't absolute, principle-based values archaic, and monolithic?

Do they work in real life? How can such principles require perfection from imperfect, finite beings like us?

If absolute values were the correct ones, why has the modern man abandoned them to subjective, relativistic ethics? Eternal principles is true that they can bring great frustration and confusion—if we fail to understand their true purpose, role, and function. After all, who can follow them without error? Principle-based values exist not to demand legalistic perfection in our conduct, as such demand would be unrealistic considering the limitations of human nature. Instead of struggling to climb the highest mountain and demand moral perfection in everything we do, absolute principles have a surprisingly *different* role to play in life.

Universal principles function as motivators to help us develop *character* through strife, persistence, and hard work. Universal principles that govern human existence are present to give to our lives direction, orientation, and the vision that will help us to be true to our selves. Stated in a different way, universal principles function like an inner compass, portraying the whole picture and journey of our lives, helping us to evaluate where are we are at any single moment, compared with where we should be. The discrepancy we sense between where we are at any stage of life with where we should be, triggers momentum and action to align "where we are at the moment" with our life's true destination and journey that would bring us genuine, sustained happiness and contentment.

The surprising different use
of fundamental laws and principles

Eternal Principles of humanity such us justice, patience, diligence, industriousness, simplicity, modesty, faithfulness and the golden rule exist to teach us understanding, sympathy, patience, forgiveness, grace, and compassion. Universal principles do not exist to demand moral perfection in us, but to *remind us* of our human limitations. It is through the awareness and recognition of *humanity's imperfect nature* that we learn wisdom, understanding, forgiveness, and good judgment. The *unchanged* wisdom of the ages remain to remind us that we are humans, that we are not perfect, that we are limited beings–that we are learners and not the rulers of life. Moreover, it is through the acknowledgment and confession of our human limitations, that true human progress becomes possible.

> Universal principles do not exist to demand moral perfection in us, but to *remind us* of our human limitations. It is through the awareness and recognition of *humanity's imperfect nature* that we learn wisdom, understanding, forgiveness, and good judgment.

Injecting Permanent Parameters to our little, inner voice

Therefore, to start removing the clutter from our inner thinking, it is essential to introduce eternal principles that will bring simplicity, clarity, and tidiness to our little, inner voice. Such cornerstones of how life operates will be *the bedrock* of the way we think; they will function like mental filters, which will enable us to manage the way we interpret events arising from the complexity of modern living–*separating reality from illusion.*

Aligning your life with the eternal principles, which govern human existence, will save you from many headaches. As soon as you start adopting deep, fundamental truths that have been tested throughout time, your inner thinking will become less argumentative, less reactive, less stubborn, less rebellious and irrational. Your little, inner voice will become more harmonious, receptive, as you will be making a major step to help you reprogramme the way you think to defeat depressive thoughts and negative, mental monologues.

So let us take the first step to make our little, inner thinking a little less relative, a little less subjective, less complex and chaotic, by introducing eternal principles about how life works–and our understanding of life will cease to be so contradictory and confusing. Let us introduce principle-based truths and laws that existed in most societies and main religions, and have been tested for thousands and thousands of years.

Derived from the wisdom of the ages, such principle-based belief systems will bring clarity, consistency, simplicity, and order to our already exhausted inner monologue. Among others, I am talking about *readopting* principle-based virtues such as honesty, courage, justice, patience, industry, simplicity, modesty, faithfulness, and the golden rule.

Such an important step will be the start in simplifying and harmonizing your inner monologue by separating illusion from reality, and truth from error. As a result, the effects of wrong thinking will be reduced, and a new compass with a new sense of direction will be established in you to redirect your thinking and future. When you begin to adopt values based on universal principles, your inner monologue will gain *a sound consciousness,* separating lies from truth, illusion from reality, and good from evil, giving you a new momentum that will bring meaning and direction to your life.

CHAPTER 4

Second Cornerstone for a Healthy 'Inner Monologue': Rediscovering your Lost Human Identity.

On You, who are you anyway?

If I ask you, "who are you?" you may respond by telling me your name–you are not your name though! If you continue describing yourself by telling me your profession, I can argue that your job is not who you are–your job is what you do to earn your daily bread. Even if you add to your description that you are American, Italian, Greek, or English, that only names your ethnicity, the country you live in, or the language you speak. Still your response does not answer adequately my question, "who are you anyway?"

The identity society gives to you. . . .

For some reasons, society and modern culture identify you by what you do, by your ethnicity, or by your physical or personality characteristics. That is not who you are though. What you do for living, where you live, your personality profile, or even how you behave is just a tiny part of your genuine, human identity. In the world we live, happiness is *narrowly* defined by good physical appearance, relationships with important people, the right career, and a good financial standing. The opposite is also true: if our life is suddenly empty of one or some of the above, we feel hopeless and we get easily depressed. In his book, *The Sensation of Being Somebody,* Maurice Wagner pinpoints this false idea about our self-concept. He says, *"Society gives us the false idea that success equals happiness and failure equals hopelessness[11]."* Nevertheless you cannot grow solely on the identity society gives you. . . .

Your authentic human identity

It has been my experience and belief that your potential for 'personal growth' as a human being is based on a <u>solid understanding</u> of who you are. Your understanding of "who you are" is the foundation for a harmonious, little, inner monologue and of course for the resulting emotional well-being and behavior. You see, popular culture has it wrong. What you do, does not determine who you are. It is the sound belief of "who you are" that shapes the rest– thoughts, feelings and actions. Your little, inner monologue will remain confused, inefficient and clogged, unless you have a clear understanding of your true human nature and identity–an identity that is true and valid–despite if you have the right job, regardless of your physical appearance, the number of past mistakes, or your financial standing.

The Truth about You–Your True Identity

The truth about you is that your worth is beyond your feelings, beyond your behavior, your heredity, or who you perceive yourself to be. You are also more valuable and separate from any talents and other good qualities you may (or may not) have. You are truly unique! Your feelings, behavior, and talents describe just a part of you, as you are much more mysterious and more complex than any given definition–just because of your human nature, your human core! Science now tells us that your brain's structure and composition is much more complex than the stars and galaxies in the known universe[12]. You are indeed a sacred being!

You are Wonderfully and . . . Fearfully made

You are inexplicably amazing even in your tragedies! The story of your life could write a tragedy much more marvelous than the writings of Euripides, Sophocles, or Shakespeare. You could be a person much more dramatic than Antigone. You are beautiful even in the way you make mistakes.

You are distinct and unique, not only because of your potential for growth and creativity, but also in *the way you make mistakes*. The way you fall into error is wonderfully magnificent. Your growth potential is also accompanied with a fearsome but *fascinating* inclination toward self-destruction. We are the only species on Earth with a tremendous potential for growth, which is also accompanied with an equally powerful capacity for error and self-destruction. No other species has this attribute–we are matchless, we are a beautiful, mysterious, sacred creation–you are mysteriously and magnificently unique–even when in error!

You are inexplicably amazing even in your tragedies! The story of your life could write a tragedy much more marvelous than the writings of Euripides, Sophocles, or Shakespeare. You could be a person much more dramatic than Antigone. As the Bible mentions, *"you are wonderfully and fearfully made."*[13] The astonishing potential part of your nature is accompanied with a magnificent, awesome disposition for self-destruction. You are indeed wonderfully, nevertheless, "fearfully" made!

Your distinct human identity and depression

I sympathize with your sufferings as I went through this type of suffering for a long, long time. In fact, I cannot claim that I have come completely through it. I have been there! I am still there coping, striving, struggling. . . . I have a good awareness about what you are going through. I can sense your pain, and I am going to do everything possible in this little book to ease your sorrow and agony by giving you the tools to defeat depressive thoughts and feelings–so you can start to hope again!

You are wonderfully and mysteriously unique person

Even in depression, you are unique, I can experience your pain greatly; yet, I cannot sense it with precision as pain is exclusive and varies from person to person. Your pain is also unparalleled–it is singular to you. Nevertheless, if you remain open to your struggle, the soreness that you go through will be the door and catalyst for a *new consciousness of who you are*–it will create in you a new insight in to what you want from life. Your pain from depression will become the tool for a life-searching and life-changing experience!

In other words, your experience of depression will motivate you to discover dimensions of yourself and talents you never thought you had. The positive side of suffering from depression is that it makes you rethink about who you are, what you are doing with your life–what is your position in the different roles of your life. Depression pressures you to revaluate your relations with significant others, resulting in better relationships–more aligned with the universal principles of life and human conduct. With the right tools, you will be empowered to rediscover yourself. If you humbly accept and collaborate with your suffering, you will end rediscovering a life with a new meaning!

Because of your uniqueness in suffering, it is essential to understand that you are not just a being, (a being amongst beings), but a Human Being. Despite the advances in modern psychology and medicine, science cannot reduce you to a concept, category, mammal–a label. Modern Psychology cannot shrink you to one of its convenient 'labels,' as science can see a part of you–not the whole person you truly are. No science in the world can correctly define your humanity and the type of suffering you are going through. Whatever definition they may give you, it is not you! You are always much more than a category or a label they try to put you in, as their perspective is relative and therefore limited. Even when depressed, your uniqueness is rare and eternal because you are a human being–of divine nature and eternal value.

No science in the world can correctly define your humanity and the type of suffering you are going through. Whatever definition they may give you, it is not you! You are always much more than a category or a label they try to put you in, as their perspective is relative and therefore limited. Even when depressed, your uniqueness is rare and eternal because you are a human being–of divine nature and eternal value. What you are is greater than what you go through–higher, much more eternal and valuable, more sacred.

✺

The Story of Dr. Viktor Frankl

Dr. Frankl, an Austrian psychiatrist, was a determinist, nurtured and educated in the 'school' of old, Freudian psychology. This Freudian branch of psychology claims that whatever happened during your childhood years (how you were brought up, in other words) shapes your entire character and personality–which governs and controls your life, past, present, and future. After the formative childhood years, the "Freudians" claim that there is not much you can do to change things, as your basic character was formed and set in like concrete when you were a child. Nevertheless, life taught a different lesson to Dr. Victor. Life instructed him the unlimited value and mystery of his humanity, which cannot be defined and put in any box by the theories he was taught at school.

Because of his Jewish background, Dr. Frankl was imprisoned in the Nazi death camps during World War II. Except his sister, his wife and parents died in the concentration camps or died to the gas ovens. Dr. Frankl himself suffered the agony of never knowing whether he would still be alive the next day, the next hour . . . the next moment. It was during his stay in the concentration camps that he discovered what he later called "the last of the human freedoms"[14]–the inner freedom to choose to be at peace with ourselves, the freedom to choose our attitude no matter of what adverse circumstances we face. Dr. Victor discovered what he did not learn from years of psychiatric practice of his deterministic Freudian discipline. He discovered his true human value and identity–when he learned that human freedom comes from within, from your mind, soul and spirit, not from your childhood, environment, or even from your genes!

He managed to cultivate the last place where he could be free–in his thoughts. He developed techniques to detach himself from the realities of his daily circumstances and liberate his mind, so he could make better decisions that would improve his adverse circumstances. He chose to be free in his mind, soul, and spirit. He developed the skills of changing his mental state from a negative–which reflected his adverse circumstances–to a positive and free one that would help him make better choices. He learned to dedramatize his little, inner monologue and therefore cultivated free, inner thinking; he developed techniques to separate himself from his circumstances and experience real inner freedom in the midst of turmoil of the Nazi concentration campus. With his imagination, he was giving imagined lectures to his imaginary students about his newly discovered theories of the human mind. He used his human imagination positively to cope with the harsh reality of the concentration camps.

In his book *"Man's Search For Meaning,"* Dr. Viktor Frankl, tell us how he survived the *tragic* circumstances of imprisonment by discovering and nurturing the true substances that make up the essence of his humanity. He did not allow the situation to infect, invade and occupy his mind and soul, because he discovered that his unique human identity and value were much greater and higher than his imprisonment and torture by the Nazis. He chose to see his *tragedy* from above–not from below–from the top and not from the bottom. He discovered his eternal value as a human being and his unique human traits that empowered him to transcend his misery into triumph. He won because he realized that his human substance and value was greater than his problems and obstacles. He learned the art of applied inner freedom.

What you are is greater than what you go through–higher, much more eternal and valuable, more sacred. When you become conscious and nurture your human genes that separate you from animals, huge problems become insignificant. They will still be there, in front of you; but, they will not have any frustrating power over you–they may still bruise but they will not crush your soul. Your awareness of your true human nature will empower your inner freedom to fight back with proactive tactics and solutions.

"They can take everything away from you," according to
Dr. Frankl, *"except your ability to view a situation
in the way you want to view it."*

It is your ability to give and apply a higher meaning to your circumstances, despite how terrible they may seem. When you approach your case with a higher meaning, attitude and perspective, pain becomes bearable, the mind less overcharged, your little, inner monologue less destructive– your inner freedom muscles will begin to grow and your vision for a meaningful life will become a reality.

Another School of thought today:

Derived from a blend of eastern religions and philosophies, another school of thought has gained popularity in today's popular culture. This new school of thought attempts to redefine human nature in a radical way. Briefly, it advocates that man possesses great powers and vast amounts of energy and intelligence. Supporters of this new school of thought claim "we have no limitations," we can become perfect beings, and it is entirely up to us to reach perfection and become . . . small gods.

Surprisingly similar to the sophists', this school of thought argues that truth is subjective; it is how we feel it with our mind and emotions. Same as the sophists of ancient Athens thought 2,400 years ago, they argue that truth is subjective, that values are not real, but merely a matter of the opinion of the individual or the culture. They in essence claim the same as the great sophist, Protagoras, who declared, *"Man is the measure of all things,"* blurring the distinction between good and evil–virtues and vices.

It is true that human beings have a vast potential of intellect, energy and brain power that wait to be utilized. That does not mean that we will use them wisely, when we eventually tap into such powers, though. We have to remind ourselves that a basic definition of wisdom is to know the limitations that define our humanity. The new school of thought advocates that we have no such limitations, as we are beings with unlimited potential. Wisdom of the ages, on the other hand, says, "I am a human being and my power and potential for real improvement is to accept, acknowledge and work within my human limitations." We are human beings and because we are humans we should accept, embrace, and work within those limitations that are part of our human genes. The awareness of our limitations is the starting point from where real growth in our human condition is possible–if we were not limited by our own nature, we would not be called 'humans' in the first place. Focusing on our strengths is essential; moreover, we have to be also aware of humanity's propensity toward self-destruction and disposition toward evil.

You are truly unique, of infinite eternal and sacred nature. Your inner freedom comes from within and it is not so much dependent on your childhood, environment, circumstances, or heredity. Your paradoxical, human nature states that you are a mysterious being with strangely beautiful behavior both in your best and worst moments. This paradox of your human distinctiveness states that you cannot separate one side of your nature from the other. You just cannot take a knife and cut your humanity into two pieces. We need to recognize and become aware of our human limitations in the light of our human potential. In the same respect, we should calculate our potential in the light of our limitations and our propensity for error. In this way, there is possibility for real wisdom and real growth for humanity. Focusing on, or ignoring one of our two traits violates the essence of our humanity, with devastating consequences in the balance and well-being in our lives.

CHAPTER 5

Third cornerstone
for a Healthy 'Inner Monologue':
Redefining Life

In our myopic, *sophistic* way of thinking, we learn to view and understand life with a possessive, cynical, and controlling attitude. "It's my life!" we affirm! " Advertising slogans are bombarding us daily through a variety of media channels, pushing us toward this type of life-style. Life, in our modern understanding, is just like a disposable item. We use and 'consume' life and we "dry out" everything in life that is good–disregarding life's sacredness and meaning. We tend to lay claim to life, treating her like a throwaway item–disregarding the sanctity of life. A good, representative example of man's egotistic view is how we have managed earth's natural resources for the last fifty years–with unfavorable consequences on the planet's climate. Indeed, man thinks life is his own object–just to realize eventually that man was the subject of life in the first place. Having ignored the laws of nature, and how life operates, we set our own subjective values of living, just to discover in the end that we were living or chasing an illusion, a lie.

The importance and sanctity of life

Contrary to popular belief, life is not our possession, it has never been, and life will not be in our ownership and under humanity's control. Life is a gift–life is a sacred, mysterious gift given from above. Just as every gift, life does not come with exclusive rights or privileges. We do not own life and *life does not owe us*. You do not own life and therefore life does not owe you! You and I have not signed a contract with the mystery gift called 'life . . .' Life comes without preconditions, stipulations, and with no provisions that are designed to serve our *short-sighted* wants and needs. Life is not humanity's servant; instead, we are the servants of life. By finding the unique way how we can contribute to life, life then becomes meaningful, satisfying our deepest needs.

The mystery of life and Existentialism

Existentialists hold the belief that life's most important questions cannot be answered. Although, not an existentialist, I confess that I agree with the above argument–we just cannot define, label, or put in a box the sacred and infinite attributes of life. There are certain things in life that science will never be able to explain through reason, or to evaluate by a scientific means. Some properties of life, whether positive or negative, just cannot be explained, since attempting to put life in a box, life loses its beauty, sacredness and meaning. .

Life is in charge–we are not

Just as we do not own life, neither do we control life! In our self-centred value system, we blind ourselves when we take life for granted, when we think that we are the masters of life, though in reality we are just *beginners* with an assigned mission to fulfill, a character to develop, and a contribution to make to the world. Clarifying my point one-step further, we are not supposed to manipulate life to fit our wants, little wishes, and short-sighted desires. Life is much larger than our limited understanding of her.

On the fairness of life: Should life always be fair with us?

Because of our controlling and egotistic attitudes, we demand life to be fair with us. If life is fair, why then do almost *"16,000 children die from hunger-related causes* every-day"[15]–while we have the resources to feed those children? To demand that life should be fair, is expressing the unhealthy attitude mentioned above, which states that life belongs to us and that we have a legal right over life–that we have the upper hand! As written in the beginning of the chapter, we never signed a contract with life–we are born into the mystery of life, and it is our assignment to find meaning in our daily circumstances.

How our attitude about life affects our little, inner monologue

In response to the inconsistent way of living our lives, our little, inner monologue is silently protesting. Instead of listening to what the small voice of our conscience is try-ing to say, we shut him off and keep on doing our 'own thing'. In the end, we tend to experience shallow self-awareness, disposable relationships, transitory friendships, and fragile marriages. The cost to our inner self-talk, when we approach our lives with a controlling, utilitarian way, is that we develop all types of insecurities, anxieties, and negative emotions–our little, inner self-talk becomes full of anxiety and fear. Attempting to manipulate life creates serious conflict between our short-sighted desires and our human conscience.

Such conflict does not just subtract from life, but also eventually wears down our little, inner monologue to a point of ineffectiveness, catastrophe, or collapse, with the real possibility of a nervous breakdown, and depression. The cause of the problem is that we have mistreated the gift of life as we have attempted to control than to embrace the mystery and sacredness of life.

What is our part then?

Instead of being reactive, we should encourage our little self-talk to respond with grace to life's difficulties, challenges, and tragedies. A wise quote says, *"Smile at life and life will smile back at you"*[16]. It is essential to understand that we gain nothing by adopting a reactive and rebellious attitude toward life. Many times people are so over reactive that instead of showing reverence to life, they even want to take revenge on life. Indeed, it has been my experience that if we take life too seriously, we will never get out of it alive. Instead of reacting to life without a vision, a purpose and long-run perspective, let's discover our mission and master the eternal principles of how life operates–then you will be empowered to play the 'game of life' with more confidence, a new sense of reality, strength, faith, and peace. Applying the rules of life makes you one-step ahead! You do not just react to life anymore–you have the ability to choose, to *proact!* Keep in mind; animals *react*, while human beings have the ability to *think* before acting. To be a little more specific; what will you gain if you sacrifice the Queen in a chess game just to capture a Soldier Pawn? Instead, avoid the temptation of reacting to the feeling of the moment and go *with confidence* for the opponent's Queen or the King–even if you have to sacrifice that little pawn.

Even when you play the game of life by abiding to the universal, unchanging principles that have been tested through ages, there will be times that you may lose a battle or two–do not get discouraged though–it does not mean the game of life is over. You may go through tragic moments in your life right now and you think that you lost your Queen! If your Queen is lost, in the chess game of life, the King is not lost unless you give up on life. The game of life is not lost until your last breath. As long as you keep on believing and hoping in life, the King is *alive* and you have the potential for victory. The key to winning the game of life is to keep in mind the overview of the game, refusing to reach conclusions about short-run failures and losses. In the end, you will reconcile yourself with life because you will learn to readjust your choices with the permanent principles of life. The person who reconciles her self with life is the one who believes in life–he/she becomes the winner of the game!

> *Our subjective value system is manifested in our inner self-talk in the form of emotional dependences–false understanding of our identity, unrealistic expectations of how life 'should be', what we are entitled from life, how life owe us, and what life still needs to give us.*

Life is a mystery; it cannot be controlled or manipulated. Even when we are aligned with life's true principles, we cannot put life in a box. The subjective views of the world with a relative value system have created an illusionary world in our mind that detaches our inner thinking from a healthy view of reality. As a result, our subjective value system is manifested in our inner self-talk in the form of emotional dependences–false understanding of our identity, unrealistic expectations of how life 'should be', what we are entitled from life, how life owe us, and what life still needs to give us.

Because of short-sighted values and beliefs, we react to life by writing a drama script and *immerse* ourselves in it–*we dramatize life, and we act upon a drama script that is not really ours.* The first step to *dedramatize* your life and your daily circumstances is to collaborate with life and find how *you best fit* in your personal challenges. You can find happiness when you align yourself with life's eternal principles, when you serve life by finding what makes you truthful, genuine human being. It is the discovery of your *unique position* in life, and how you can contribute to life that will make you happy and fulfilled.

> *"Ultimately, man should not ask what the meaning of his life is, but rather must recognize that it is he who is asked. In a word, each man is questioned by life; and he can only answer to life by answering for his own life; to life he can only respond by being responsible."*[17]
> *In Man's Search for Meaning, Viktor Frankl p.172*

Introduction to the Method of the Book

During the last three chapters, together, we have set the three cornerstones that contribute to a healthy inner monologue. We have redefined and rediscovered the foundations of the method of the book–Truth, your Human Identity, and your Life's mystery. In the chapter that follows, *we will bring to surface* your Personal, Emotional Dependence, and describe how it influences your every thought, feeling, and conduct. Your personal, emotional dependence is a sign of an enslaved inner monologue. It is manifested behind every clouded thought, and prevents us from making free, healthful choices.

Equipped with what your emotional dependence means to you, *I will help you to use it* in the five-step method to start neutralizing clouded, negative thoughts. In the chapters that follow, you will learn how to neutralize emotionally charged thoughts, setting your inner monologue free from the gravity of your emotional dependence, which is manifested in depressive thoughts. Such awareness of your hidden emotional dependence will empower you to make real choices based on reality, based on who you really are, based on your genuine self.

CHAPTER 6

Understanding, Defining, and Naming Your Personal, Emotional Dependence

Before explaining the five-step method in this book, we need to understand *thoroughly* what we mean by "Personal Emotional Dependence." Once you understand the type and origin of your main Emotional Dependence, I will teach you how to trace, identify and <u>name</u> your *own* unique, Emotional Dependence–that clouds your inner monologue, your inner thinking, and consequently the way you act in life.

When you clarify in your mind and heart your unique Emotional Dependence, and when you give it an appropriate name, it will be a major, practical step toward a healthier inner monologue. Such new awareness will gradually sets your little, inner self-talk free from clotted, negative thinking and the respective behavior that makes you depression-prone–with this tool at hand, your way of thinking will not be the same ever again!

Compared to the other chapters, this is the most valuable chapter in the book. It is the most significant one. This chapter is intrinsically the soul of the book because in it you will clearly understand how to define and clarify:

a) What we mean by "Personal Emotional Dependence."
b) What Emotional Dependence means personally to you.
c) How to trace your "PED," Identify it, and Name it.

Do not worry that you may get confused, as I will clarify things as clearly as possible. In fact, it has been my custom in writing to reiterate the same ideas using different words, in order for you to gain a sound comprehension and understanding of this important concept, so it will make a difference in your self-talk, improving greatly your little, inner monologue.

So now, let us define what "Personal Emotional Dependence" means, what it means to you, and how you can trace it, identify it, and name it:

Definition of Personal Emotional Dependence:

"Personal Emotional Dependence" is an image, person, relationship, remembrance, hope, or dream that brings intimacy, deep feelings of affection, romance, and closeness (warmth) of heart. It is any remembrance that could give or could have given meaning to the very existence of our being; nonetheless, life, unfavorable circumstances and adversities refused to provide for it, or may have taken it away from us. Your "Personal Emotional Dependence" could have been the loving mother or father that suddenly died or left you; it may have been the best-loved pet during your childhood; a loving relationship with your soul mate, which for whatever reason ended unexpectedly; it could also be the ideal career

you were so passionate about but you suddenly lost, or one of your dreams that never came to fruition.

"Personal Emotional Dependence" is unique and different from person to person. It could be the loving relationship you never experienced, or one you lost . . . a key personal characteristic you really think you are lacking . . . a mental or a physical limitation you have carried with you since you were born; a desired goal such as a college degree which for whatever reason you could not earn . . . the sudden loss of a loved one you were so depended on, or the loss of a job you really enjoyed. It can be the longing for your dream career, or the longing for the ideal companion that would satisfy all your emotional and romantic needs.

You may not have realized or even remembered well what happened years ago–during your childhood years. Nevertheless, your Personal Emotional Dependence has been crystallized in time deep into your subconscious–becoming from conscious and specific thought to subconscious and vague.

Personal Emotional Dependence:
An easily remembered definition

Your Personal Emotional Dependence is an object, a person, or relationship–any remembrance that brings deep feelings of affection, romance, and closeness (warmth) of heart, which you believed would have given meaning to the very existence of your being.

A scientific definition of your 'Personal Emotional Dependence':

Although a complex definition of the PED is beyond the scope of this book, a scientific definition of Personal Emotional Dependence is that it is *the longing and cries of unmet needs during childhood years*[18]. *The <u>wounded child in us</u> that always wants, longs, cries, gets angry, and the child in us remains hurt, critical and unsatisfied because few of us have had a perfect childhood.*

ෙ෧

A word of caution: 'Personal Emotional Dependence' does not have the same meaning as the general term of 'Emotional Dependence.'

The general definition of emotional dependence is getting one's good feelings compulsively from the outside world. It means needing to be emotionally filled from outside rather than from inside. PED on the other hand, is the lack of inner freedom from a void created *in us*. It is our subconscious unwillingness to "let go" of our unique, 'Personal Emotional Dependence.' Our unique PED goes much deeper than any ordinary emotional dependence, as it is the big void created inside us because of . . . *that loving relationship we never experienced, or have lost . . . the lack of a good father of mother, a key personal characteristic we think we are lacking, a physical limitation we may have, or a college degree (for whatever reason) we could not earn. Your personal emotional dependence is the greatest longing in your heart that only YOU know and fully understand.*

Naming your Personal Emotional Dependence

By identifying and naming your Personal Emotional Dependence, you *transfer* vague subconscious memories and feelings into the world of conscious existence–into your conscious mind–a place where it can be recognized, understood for what it is, and handled correctly.

Why naming it? Once identified, what is the benefit in taking the time to give a name to your Personal Emotional Dependence? The answer is that the human brain needs to NAME something before it becomes REAL. Before something is named, it does not exist, because either our awareness of it is too dim, or because we have not noticed or quantified it yet–consequently, we think that it might as well not be there. Although PED is powerfully present in our little, inner monologue, Personal Emotional Dependence was primarily formed in childhood. Since many years have elapsed, our Personal Emotional Dependence has been buried deep in our subconscious, changing form from conscious and particular to a form that is now subconscious and vague. By identifying and naming your Personal Emotional Dependence, you *transfer* vague subconscious memories and feelings into the world of conscious existence–into your conscious mind–a place where it can be recognized, understood for what it is, and handled correctly.

Before selecting the name of your Personal Emotional Dependence, it is essential to remind yourself that your major emotional dependence is unique: *It is the remembrance of that object, memory, relationship, or person, which/who brings you deep feelings of affection, feelings of romance, closeness (warmth) of heart, triggering a meaning to every fiber of your existence. . . .* Consequently, the NAME of your personal emotional dependence should instantly *bring to mind* those same feelings of warmth and deep feelings of closeness of heart. . . .

How to Trace your Personal Emotional Dependence

The idea is to find a name that will *connect* you with your childhood–to connect you with the innocent and beautiful emotions *you once felt as a child.* Although now we are grown-ups, we still have images and memories from our childhood that bring us the intense feelings of intimacy that we once experienced when we were children. Pick the strongest remembrance that brings such rich feelings of emotions from you childhood–*feelings derived from childhood that are full of vibrancy, love, acceptance, hope, and understanding.* Then, all you have to do is <u>give it a relevant name</u> so that each time you bring it to mind, these emotions are aroused again.

To reiterate this once more, *your Personal Emotional Dependence can be the name of an object, person, or relationship, or even a moment. It could be a cherished moment when all the family were having fun at home, when you were at your best and everything looked marvelous. It could be the name of your first teddy bear, the name of your hiding place. It could be the name of the person who made a difference to your childhood. Finally yet importantly, it could be just your favorite dog, or other pet, which you still cherish and remember with nostalgia–regardless how many years have gone by.*

Although not limited to your childhood, memories of your adulthood are built on your childhood experiences and therefore they also can arouse such profound intimate feelings. It could be the first romantic love, the first kiss, or the unforgettable excitement you felt from catching your first fish . . . or the salary you got from your first job. Such memories are embedded in our subconscious so deeply that their revival always triggers intense feelings of closeness and intimacy. All you have to do is just choose the greatest of these memories and subsequently give it a name.

Go ahead and _choose a name_ from the most cherished moments of your life–even if it brings tears to your eyes. You may even imagine, or dream a scenario you always wanted to experience–then just *label it* with the name of your choice. Give it a name that will respect and reflect your desire and the eagerness for it. It does not matter whether the situation is real or a fictional, or whether it has taken place in the past.

Practical tips for Naming your Personal Emotional Dependence:

Hence, take your time when choosing *your PED name.* Think with your head although above all, *think with your heart* in selecting the right *name* for your Personal Emotional Dependence. A good idea is to go close to nature and test the name you have chosen. If the name is not simple, funny, and aligned with the simplicity, fullness, and beauty of the trees, of the sea, of the forest . . . then change it and choose a name that does. What I am giving you are not strict rules, but a set of principles you can creatively change and experiment. *The murmuring of the wind, and the soothing sound of wave should tell you if the name you have chosen is the right one for you. . . .*

Preferably (but not exclusively) the name of your PED can sound like a nickname. Although the name of your Personal Emotional Dependence must be significant to you, you can "nickname" it by making it shorter, simpler, and funnier. As the goal of this book is to teach you to *de-dramatize* cloudy thinking, a funny, cute or just plain weird name of your PED will make a difference.

If you still have trouble selecting your PED name, a practical way would be to search the Internet and get into web sites of baby-names, ancient names, or even pet-names, and pick a name that is suitable for *what you cherish—memories of a person, relationship, object , a name that best connects you with the longings of your heart!*

❧❧

<u>I have chosen *"Oúhou-oúhou"* to *name* my Personal Emotional Dependence</u> as it resembles the *first vocal sounds babies make when they express curiosity, gratification, and satisfaction when exploring the new world around them.* It is the sound babies make before learning to talk, sounds of wonder, curiosity, understanding and satisfaction. It took me almost two months to choose my PED name, because of the great importance it has in the implementation of the five-step method, the simple method described in this book. <u>From now and on, I will use the term Personal Emotional Dependence and "personal *Oúhou-oúhou*" interchangeably in an attempt to escape from academic definitions and present the PED in a practical, meaningful, even humorous way.</u>

> *From now and on, I will use the term Personal Emotional Dependence and the term 'personal Oúhou-oúhou' interchangeably, in my attempt to escape from formal academic definitions and present the PED in a more understandable, and practical way.*

Once you have decided on the name of your *'personal Oúhou-oúhou'*, please *write it down* as we are going to use it in the chapters that follow.

> ### *Your PED Name Declaration:*
> The name of my Personal Emotional Dependence
> (my personal *Oúhou-oúhou*), the *name* that brings
> me intense memories and deep feelings of affection,
> feelings of romance, closeness and warmth of heart,
> triggering meaning to every fiber of my being is
>
> _______________________________.

In the following chapter, we will describe the three drama scripts we enact in daily life, in our desperate attempt to fulfil our Personal Emotional Dependence (our personal *Oúhou-oúhou*). Because of the great void Personal Emotional Dependence has created, we will describe the three major ways *we react to life* in desperation to fill this void–the void in our Personal Emotional Dependence. Once the three principal ways of your reactive behavior are revealed in front of your eyes, we will use the five steps to analyze and eventually change such reactive thinking–for a better, *proactive* thought and action.

CHAPTER 7

Three Drama Scripts People Play

*'Personal Emotional Dependence' and
The Three Drama Scripts it creates.*

*PED creates a big void in the most potentially creative–
and at the same time–the most destructive instrument, the
human heart. In our attempt to fill this void, we reactively
engage in one of the three drama scripts.*

Now that you have a clear understanding of what 'Personal Emotional Dependence' is, and what it means to you, let us examine further, why it is so important in shaping our little, inner monologue, and therefore in determining our daily conduct. Personal Emotional Dependence is not just a feeling, or an event that took place a long time ago. PED creates a big void in the most potentially creative–and at the same time–the most destructive instrument, the human heart. In our attempt to fill this void, we *reactively* engage in one of the three drama scripts we are going to examine in this chapter.

In other words, you and I are *glued* to Personal Emotional Dependence (glued to our personal *Oúhou-oúhou*)! In desperation to fill the void deep in our souls, we act on one of the three primary drama scripts, narrowing in this way our field of vision of the world, making us helpless, depressed prisoners. A limited view of life with fewer choices is how Personal Emotional Dependence (our personal *Oúhou-oúhou*) is manifested in our life. Now, let us explain in detail the *three principal drama scripts* we play out compulsively and reactively in our attempt to fill the void in our Personal Emotional Dependence (our personal *Oúhou-oúhou*):

First Personal Emotional Dependence Drama Script: The "Loser" drama script

The Loser drama script describes people who exhibit a "they-took-it-from-me" *loser* attitude. We blame others and life because of unfavorable circumstances. We complain about life's unfairness toward us, and our victimized attitude, as a result, prevents us from making the choices that would improve our daily living. We have a conviction that life deprived us of something very important that could have made us both fulfilled and happy. We feel that we were entitled to receiving all the best life could give; nevertheless, life has just failed to provide it to us. We think that it is life's fault as it was life's responsibility to give us what we wanted, what we thought could have made us fulfilled and alive.

Many times, our perception of how life has treated us makes us shy, lonely, reactive, critical, and hypersensitive; other times, having nothing to expect from life, we become rebellious, complaining and blaming people and circumstances of how unfair they have treated us. Feeling victimized, deep down in heart, people in this "it-is-your-fault" drama script wait for something to happen, someone to take care of them, expecting for someone else to make things happen and provide a solution to their problems. The "Loser" play is the most noticeable drama script as the augmented "inner child" is evident in these persons–it is the little boy or the little girl that has been forgotten, betrayed and abandoned by everybody and desperately waits for something good to happen.

The little, inner monologue of the "Loser" drama script

"Life is not fair; Life owes me happiness; instead, life has deceived me. I was supposed to have the upper hand in life; instead, I am forgotten and abandoned without any person to help me get out of my desperate circumstances."

Unaware of the mystery and sacredness of life, the "loser" attitude of this drama script is rooted in the *false conviction* that we *own* life and therefore we are entitled to all life can give. In this drama script, we see life to be like any other commodity that is meant to be consumed, and satisfy our needs.

Having formed *false convictions* of how life "should" be, we feel betrayed, as we are not conscious how the laws and principles of life operate. To escape from this drama script, we have to become *conscious* that *we do not own life*, and therefore *life does not owe us*. We have never signed a contract with life–life comes with no preconditions, stipulations, requirements, and assumptions to meet our shortsighted needs and wants. We have to recondition our egotistic little, inner monologue that life is not our servant; instead, we have to take practical steps to learn how to reposition ourselves and *serve life*–because serving life is the same as *serving our own deepest needs*.

Rectifying the little, inner monologue of the "Loser" drama script:

Because this is the first exercise in the book, here are the instructions on how to complete it:

–First, *reiterate* what Personal Emotional Dependence means to you:

–Second, complete the exercise by reading the *corrected little, inner monologue* by filling it with your PED name, whenever there is an <u>underlined</u> blank space. The exercises that follow are easy to complete, as they require just your attention and your PED name (Your personal *Oúhou-oúhou* name)–the name of your Personal Emotional Dependence.

Correcting the little, inner monologue of the "Loser" drama script

A. Before starting to correct the little, inner monologue of the "Loser" drama script, first let us review your Personal Emotional Dependence:

The <u>name</u> of my Personal Emotional Dependence (the name of my personal Oúhou-oúhou), the name that brings me intense memories and deep feelings of affection, feelings of romance, closeness and warmest of heart, triggering meaning to every cell of my being is ________________________.

B. Second, read carefully the *new, adjusted inner monologue* and fill in the <u>underlined space</u> with the name of your PED, (<u>the name of your personal Oúhou-oúhou</u>).
After completing the exercise that replaces the inner monologue of the "Loser" drama script with the *correct* little, inner voice, *reread the new little, monologue couple of times* until you become conscious of the new, healthful life script, which is now *free* from your Personal Emotional Dependence (free from your personal Oúhou-oúhou).

Adjusting the little, inner voice of the "Loser" drama script:

"Life does not owe me my ____________. At times, I feel strongly that life took away my ____________. Nevertheless, I remind myself that I was not entitled to my ____________ in the first place. I came in this life owning nothing and I will return carrying nothing with me. Moreover, I realize that I am a student of life and not the owner. Therefore, I am no longer angry at life, as life has not taken my ____________(my personal Oúhou-oúhou) as I was not the owner of it in the first place.

"Instead of living with the "loser" conviction that life took away my________________(my personal Oúhou-oúhou), I choose to move forward and find new meaning and contentment by aligning my wants and needs with the eternal laws of life—by living a principle-based life—a life with simplicity and purpose.

I set aside my ________________(my personal Oúhou-oúhou), so I can rewrite a new life script by finding ways to contribute to life. I assert that is what life wants from me that will give meaning–not what I desire from life. Life has given me a rare set of combination of talents and abilities. My human composition is unique and my potential to serve life is also unique–I can contribute to life the way no one else can. I am a distinct human being and life demands my unique contribution. I am not enslaved to my ____________ (my personal Oúhou-oúhou) any longer! Life depends on me to complete my mission, as it is a mission that only I can fulfill!

Second Personal Emotional Dependence Drama Script: The "Hunter" Drama script

The "Hunter" drama script entangles people who are always up to something. In a subconscious quest for *"intimacy, deep feelings of affection, romance, and warmest of heart . . ."* such persons are actively pursuing careers, and endlessly set higher standards to accomplish. They are usually competitive personalities. On a quest for an illusionary world that will satisfy the longings of their heart, people trapped in the "Hunter" drama script have high expectations for material possessions, career, relationships, and social status.

People playing the "Hunter" drama can be an "ends justify the means" persons as they enjoy work–but not the people around them. Such driven personalities are *restless, impatient, and demanding,* with many unnecessary stressors and anxieties attached to them. Persons who fall under this drama script have difficulty accepting themselves. They tend to be eager, anxious, as they have not learned how to slow down and be at peace with themselves. Such persons seem unable to appreciate and taste the simple pleasures of life, as in their head, there is a constant noise, an inner, little voice that commands them to go for the *next goal, the next achievement, the next girlfriend or boyfriend,* hoping that *this time* will be the one they were looking for in life. Hunters are good candidates of "Burned-out-caused" depression because of poor stress management yent as they are seldom happy with what they have achieved already–they aim endlessly for the next goal, the next project, the next relationship–hoping that the next achievement will indeed bring fulfillment in life.

People who are easily trapped in this drama script resemble the story of "Tantalus"[19] from Greek mythology. After having committed some serious crimes against the gods, Tantalus's punishment was to stand in a pool of water beneath a fruit tree with low branches. Whenever he reached for the fruit, the branches raised the fruit of his grasp. Whenever he bent down to get a drink, the water receded before he could drink. In short, both Tantalus and the Hunter drama script *were cursed* for eternally being tempted and enticed, without real satisfaction, contentment, and peace.

Lack of contentment

The central attribute of the "Hunter" drama script is *lack of contentment*. Once a set of goals and aspirations are met, anxious hunters set higher goals to *pursue*, because the last achievement did not fill the void in their Personal Emotional Dependence (the void in their personal *Oúhou-oúhou*).

Whether related to career goals, relationships, or social status aspirations, people engaged in the "Hunter" drama script think they know what they want *"this time"* and *"certainly"* how to get there, hoping they will attain true happiness and contentment that will fill the void in their heart. This time, *they think,* they will hunt down what is missing in their life, which would bring them true happiness, *"intimacy, deep feelings of affection, romance, and warmth of heart . . . ."*

The little, inner monologue of the "Hunter" Drama Script

The inner monologue of the "Hunter" drama script whispers, *"I will be happy and relaxed when I attain this . . ."* or *"I will feel good when I find a lover who meets my expectations,"* Or *"I will feel ok when I acquire this level of success"*, or *"I will feel satisfied when I achieve this social status . . . ."* *"This time, I know what I want"* and *"certainly"* how to get there! They think.

In reality, they are caught in a vicious hunting circle of desperate attempts to fill the void in heart with . . . the next promotion, the next relationship, the next achievement, a bigger house, a newer car. . . . As a result, people engaged in the "Hunter" drama script *rarely* experience satisfaction and contentment with who they are and what they have achieved already.

Many times, the inner monologue of the hunter drama script takes a more subtle form such as, *"I will be happy and relaxed when I pay off my mortgage . . .", "when I finish this project . . .", "when my children are settled . . .", "I will be at peace when I retire . . . ."* However, the hunter drama script engages people into a vicious cycle as they rarely experience contentment and peace with what they have achieved already–as such persons forget that enjoying the ride between goals is also important and fulfilling.

Correcting the little, inner monologue of
the Hunter drama script

First, let us review your Personal Emotional Dependence: *The name of my Personal Emotional Dependence (the name of my personal Oúhou-oúhou), the name that brings me intense*

*memories and deep feelings of affection, feelings of romance, close-
ness and warmth of heart, triggering meaning to every cell of my
being is ________________.*

Second, The self-talk of the hunter drama can be rectified by
adopting the following little, thinking loop:

*I understand that when I see myself moving from goal to
goal, from relationship to relationship, from pleasure to pleasure,
without lasting satisfaction, the "Hunter" drama kicks in. I recognize that I compulsively enact the "Hunter" drama, because of
my subconscious need to fill the void in my ________________, in my
personal Oúhou-oúhou–the emptiness in my Personal Emotional
Dependence.*

*I realize that my 'Hunter' tendency to aim continually at
higher goals comes from the impulse to fill the great emptiness in
my personal emotional dependence, my ________________the void in
my personal Oúhou-oúhou– the one that I 'think' will bring deep
feelings of affection, feelings of romance, closeness and warmth of
heart, thus triggering a meaning to every fiber of my being.*

*I now understand that my engagement in the 'Hunter' drama
play, in essence, is a play that is illusory, foreign to my needs,
which detaches me from reality. Now, I am becoming conscious
that my endless aim at goals, objectives or relationships, does not
fill the vacuum of my ________________, my Personal Emotional
Dependence (my personal Oúhou-oúhou).*

*The "Hunter" drama script does not determine my true human
identity and worth. My precious worth as a human being will not
change by achieving the next goal, getting the next promotion, or
by meeting the next set of expectations, because such conduct is*

a part of the Hunter script, a script that is played reactively and compulsively–detaching me from my feelings and preventing me from enjoying life right now.

I refuse to engage in the "Hunter" drama, as I am no longer tight up to my ___________ (my personal Oúhou-oúhou). I accept myself as a unique, sacred human being, and I refuse to be at the mercy of my ______________. I acknowledge and cherish my worth as a human being, without having to run from relationship to relationship, from accomplishment to accomplishment to fill the void of my ___________ as I am an accepted and worthy person as I am.

The 'Hunter' drama script limits our inner freedom to make sound choices in our daily conduct. It humiliates human nature, as living in this drama script does not consider our genuine needs and precious value as human beings.

Third Personal Emotional Dependence Drama Script: The "Narcissist" Drama Script.

People *entangled* in the "Narcissist" drama script are often "happy" people, or people who think they 'have it all' in life. Many times, they are persons whom talents society holds in high esteem. Such persons are characterized by high expertise in medicine, science, business, or in the field of fine arts such as singing, dance, or theatre. Often, they are brilliant minds with tremendous capabilities, talents, and skills in their profession. They are so good at what they do, that their "high-in-demand" expertise is the *center* of interest, focus, and care in life. Whether serving a passionate career, relationship, a hobby, or any other activity, the persons enacting the "Narcissist" drama script are *consumed* by their passion. At the end, they grow to be so self-consumed with it that they have become *indifferent* to what is going on beyond their "little, wonderful world." In essence, they have created a golden cage that becomes an idol and object of worship.

The little *utopia world* in which people of this drama script operate is the object that gives meaning to their lives. Eventually their passion becomes an idol, a 'god,' an object they passionately value . . . and worship. They think that the void in their Personal Emotional Dependence (in their personal *Oúhou-oúhou*) is filled and every need is met–*they have found their personal Oúhou-oúhou,* or so they think!

The predicament is that persons who operate with this drama script develop such a consuming passion that they *ignore* the other roles in life. Engaging in this type of drama script *costs people too much*, though at first they do not realize the high price they will have to pay. Their passion becomes their primary *affection* so everything else in life orbits around it, with less priority and significance. The element of *role imbalance* in such persons is evident, *as what they do is all what they are*–their passion is the *only role and identity* they recognize in life. The rest of life's roles, either have low importance or serve to keep the person entangled in this meaningless, drama.

Although it may not be so obvious drama in people, in comparison with the "Loser" and the "Hunter" drama plays, the "Narcissist" drama script is by far the most *dangerous* drama script. When the person's little, *utopia castle* goes through a sudden demolition, they fall into severe depression–when the little utopia for whatever reason, collapses, *they crumble with it as well!*

Examples of this drama script are corporate executives who jump out of the window because their business is ruined, as well as ordinary people who just cannot recover from the loss of a significant relation. This drama is indeed the most subtle drama of the three, as people trapped in it *are so consumed* by their high-in-demand talent, relationship, or activity that they become *Narcissists*, egocentric and as a result, *they lose perspective and consciousness of the total picture of where life is heading.* Until it is too late, they are so deeply self-absorbed in the little, utopian world that they seldom realize that something may be wrong with the other roles in their life.

In Greek mythology, *Narcissus's* obsessive love with his reflection in a pool of water finally led to his death[20]. The self-absorption with just one dimension or role in life brings *imbalance* to the other roles we have to serve. Since life consists of more than one role, successful living lies in balancing those roles harmoniously–without allowing one role to compete at the expense of the other. There is no question that we should be passionate about our work, our relationships–even our hobbies. The "Narcissist" drama script kicks in, however, when one role in our lives *dominates* the other roles.

In an extreme manifestation of the Narcissistic drama script, people become so passionate with a single tree, and therefore, have little view of the entire "forest," or the other important roles they have to serve to be complete human beings. Moreover, all other roles in their life such as spouse, parent, etc, become tools to *support* the hobby, person, activity, or job that resembles so much their Personal Emotional Dependence (their personal *Oúhou-oúhou*). The other roles in their life become necessary *sacrifices* to support the narcissistic, egotistic, self-consumed behavior.

Rectifying the "Narcissist" drama play

Same as the previous exercises, all you have to do is read carefully the text, and just fill in the <u>underlined space</u> with the <u>*name*</u> of your Personal, Emotional Dependence (the name of your personal *Oúhou-oúhou*)

First, let's review briefly your Personal Emotional Dependence:

The name of my Personal Emotional Dependence, the name that brings to me intense memories and deep feelings of affection, feelings of romance, closeness and warmth of heart, triggering meaning to every cell of my being is _____________

Adjusting the inner monologue of the "Narcissist" drama script

When I lose touch with reality, and when I experience false contentment by passionately focusing in a relationship or an activity that is so time-and energy-consuming, I operate under the "Narcissist" drama. I recognize that I engage in this drama script because of my subconscious need to fill the void in my _______________, (in my personal Oúhou-oúhou).

When I engage myself in this script, I may feel that all my needs are fulfilled and that I have found my _______________. Actually, though, feeding on this drama, I live an illusion, a utopia, a lie! My ___________(my personal Oúhou-oúhou) is not met just by focusing passionately on a single activity, person, or relationship. In real life, it is the balancing of the roles I have to play that brings real fulfillment, peace, and happiness.

I am conscious now that I am not my passion and the passion is not me. Because of my precious, human identity, my value is greater than my _____________ (my personal Oúhou-oúhou) that activates in my passion. I choose to stop playing this script as this drama motivates me to live an illusion, a lie, which is not other than my attempt to fill the void of my _______________ (the emptiness created in my personal Oúhou-oúhou). Every time I become conscious that I am entangled in this drama play, it no longer has power over me, as I exercise my free will, and choose not to continue in a drama script that can destroy my life.

☙❧

What the three Drama Scripts Have in Common?

The first drama script, the 'Loser,' describes people who *think* have lost hope in life–they lost all hope to fill the void in their Personal Emotional Dependence (to satisfy the void in their personal *Oúhou-oúhou*). People who enact the 'Hunter' drama script *chase and pursue* activities to fill the void of their Personal Emotional Dependence, while the third drama script, describes 'Narcissist' persons who *think* they have *satisfied* the void created by their Personal Emotional Dependence (they think, they have satisfied the emptiness of their personal *Oúhou-oúhou*).

Living an Illusion

What people in the three drama scripts *have in common* is that they *act on an illusion*. While the first drama script portrays people who experience *deprivation of an illusion*, people trapped in the second drama script *chase after an illusion*, while the third drama script describes people *living in an illusion*. Furthermore, people who operate in any one of the three drama scripts, are *dependent personalities*, individuals who are at high risk to suffer from clinical depression and the horrible symptoms that go with it.

So, What's your Drama Script?

Daily, we enact all of the three drama scripts interchangeably; nevertheless, there is a *principal drama script* that drives and dominates our life, our little, inner monologue, and consequently our daily conduct.

So, What's your favorite drama play? Which one of the three drama scripts, your Personal Emotional Dependence (your personal *Oúhou-oúhou*) pushes you to play compulsively? What is your life's dominant drama script? Are you a *Hunter*, a *Self-consumed*, seemingly content person, or a *Loser*, a person who lost all hope? Although in daily life, we enact the three principal drama scripts interchangeably, there is a *primary drama play,* which drives and dominates your little, inner monologue, your daily conduct, and therefore your life.

Any of the three principal drama scripts exhibits a "depression-prone" individual. Such persons are *glued* on their PED (they are "fixed" on their personal *Oúhou-oúhou*). Because of the *vainness* of the three drama scripts, people who are trapped in any one of the drama become *dependent personalities*–they are individuals who are at high risk to suffer from clinical depression and the painful symptoms that go with it.

Until we learn to identify and neutralize cloudy thoughts that originate in *Personal Emotional Dependence* (in our personal *Oúhou-oúhou*), we are *doomed* to fall into the trap of one of the three principal drama scripts described in this chapter. When we engage in one of the three drama scripts, we are *enslaved. We behave in a manner that is not us, our way, our mission.* Enacting any of the three drama plays restrains the inner freedom in us, limiting our options, which are necessary for living a meaningful life, preventing us from living life to the fullest.

CHAPTER 8

What our Drama Script is doing to our life

Because we are *subconsciously* glued on Personal Emotional Dependence (glued on our personal *Oúhou-oúhou*), our self-talk is flooded with thoughts of fear, passivity, insecurity, selfishness, cynicism, over ambition, vanity, and egocentrism. Our infected little, inner monologue reacts to such cloudy thoughts by *dramatizing* our daily conduct–*by engaging us in one of the three principal drama scripts.*

Reality and your favorite drama script

After you have recognized your principal drama script, let us clarify the *nature* of Personal Emotional Dependence (our personal *Oúhou-oúhou*). The void created by Personal Emotional Dependence results in the *absence* of inner freedom as PED detaches us from a healthy view of the world–*it distorts our view of reality.* PED (our Personal *Oúhou-oúhou*) generates cloudy thoughts in our little, inner self-talk–thoughts of fear, passivity, insecurity, over ambition, selfishness, cynicism, vanity, and egocentrism. In turn, the infected little, inner voice *reacts* to such cloudy thoughts by *dramatizing* our daily conduct–*by enslaving us into one of the three drama scripts*.

Because we are fixed on our *illusory Personal Emotional Dependence* (our personal *Oúhou-oúhou*), we do not enjoy a healthy understanding of reality. Our options are limited, inner freedom is limited, and therefore the ability to make choices for improvement is diminished. We are *enslaved* to Personal Emotional Dependence (tied to our personal *Oúhou-oúhou*) and the drama script it activates. We are hooked, needy on and–subconsciously–enslaved by the longings of our childhood. We are at the mercy of that person, relationship, memory, hope, (true or imaginary), that brings us intimacy, deep feelings of affection, romance, and closeness of heart. We are *bonded and tied* on the illusion of what life could be, or what life could have given us.

First Self-Talk Exercise: Learning to let go. . . .

Same with previous exercises, please read carefully the text and fill in the <u>underlined space</u> with the *name* of your Personal Emotional Dependence (the name of your personal *Oúhou-oúhou*). So, it is now your turn to *personalize* the above beliefs by playing the following little, inner monologue in your mind:

When I am glued on my ______________ (my personal *Oúhou-oúhou*), my sense of reality is like 'tunnel vision.' A Limiting view of the world is what my ___________ (my *Oúhou-oúhou*) is bringing to my life. I am *bonded and tied* on the illusion of what life could be, or what life could have given me-ignoring reality in this way.

My _____________ (personal *Oúhou-oúhou*) is also manifested in my *unwillingness* to "let go" of what I always wanted in life. It creates a *denial* to accept what life has already given me, *a denial to accept reality.* Such a refusal of not *accepting* what life has already given me, and *acting on a drama script based on what life would have been*; nevertheless, makes me a hypocrite, an actor who acts on one of the three main drama scripts.

I realize that it is the bond with my _______________(my personal *Oúhou-oúhou*) that compulsively pushes me to play one of the three drama plays. It is the person, relationship, memory, hope, true or imaginary, that brings *me* intimacy, deep feelings of affection, romance, and closeness (warmth) of heart . . ."–that pushes me to *dramatize* my life by enacting my principal drama script as I am not willing to let go of my _____________ (my personal *Oúhou-oúhou*).

Whether we enact the "Loser," the "Hunter," or the "Narcissist" drama script, we are destined to act out a drama in life that is not our, as it is a play <u>*alien to our personality and uniqueness*</u>. Regardless what drama dominates our life, we are deprived of one building block that can make us revive again–the principal attribute of a healthful personality–that is *inner freedom*.

Dedramatization

The three principal drama scripts we engage in life are elusive, full of fear, vanity, selfishness and anxiety, demoralizing and enslaving the human soul.

As the three principal drama scripts are elusive, full of fear, vanity, selfishness and anxiety, <u>demoralizing and enslaving the human soul,</u> the goal of this book is to teach you how to *dedramatize* and "Let Go" of your PED (your personal *Oúhou-oúhou*). Your Personal Emotional Dependence (*your Oúhou-oúhou*) is the reason why you compulsively dramatize your life. Moreover, when you learn to identify cloudy thoughts in your little, inner monologue that motivate you to initiate a drama script, you can begin to increase your awareness and, consequently, gain the ability to make *choices* that will empower you to *stop acting* on the three, unhealthy drama scripts, and choose to follow your true life script.

Taking responsibility for our Personal Emotional Dependence

Taking responsibility for *our* Personal Emotional Dependence, means *recognizing* that cloudy thinking in the little, inner monologue in our head comes from our *subconscious bond* with our Personal Emotional Dependence (our personal *Oúhou-oúhou*). Moreover, cloudy thoughts are generated because of our subconscious *refusal* to accept reality and build on it. Cloudy depressive thinking floods our little self-talk, because of our *subconscious denial* to start with reality, from point zero, from scratch, and to move gradually toward the life we always wanted.

Second Self-Talk Exercise:

Same with previous exercises, read carefully the text and fill in the <u>underlined space</u> with just the *name* of your Personal Emotional Dependence. So, it is now your turn to *personalize* what we have just said–by playing in your mind the following little, inner monologue:

Cloudy thoughts of inadequacy, anxiety, fear, passivity, vanity, egocentrism, and self-absorption *fuel* my engagement in the chief drama script I adopt in life–a drama that comes from my _______________ (my personal *Oúhou-oúhou*). The drama script I engage in daily conduct, is activated by cloudy thinking–thoughts that are coming from the void created by my _______________ (my personal *Oúhou-oúhou*).

Moreover, Cloudy thoughts originate from *my attachment* to my _______________ (my Personal *Oúhou-oúhou*). Cloudy thinking creates a distorted, little self-talk in me, that pushes me to enact my principal drama script that dominates my life. By *understanding* and *detecting* the source of such thoughts, which is no other than my ___________ (my personal *Oúhou-oúhou*), and work to *neutralize* such cloudy thinking, I am on my way to *create* my own true life script! Emotional freedom then, becomes *possible* that will bring in positive changes in my life.

જ

Neutralizing Cloudy Thoughts–The Aim of this little book

When we learn to neutralize cloudy thoughts, then we become response-able. We can learn to amuse and set aside distorted thinking that originates at our Personal Emotional Dependence. Applying the five-steps of the method as described in the NEXT chapter, will make a huge difference in your little, inner monologue, which will be a liberating cata-lyst to your inner freedom, your behavior and relationships.

> When we learn to neutralize cloudy thoughts,
> then we become response-able. We can learn to amuse
> and set aside distorted thinking that originates at our
> Personal Emotional Dependence.

I am not a surrealist, or even a realist. Such people accept the reality of circumstances, having no hope, a dream, or a vision for improvement. Healthy human beings just cannot live without hope, a vision, and dreams for gradual, posi-tive change. On the contrary, to be human is to have a hope a vision and a dream in the middle of difficulties and daily challenges. I have become a hopeful person learning to fight depression–learning to create inner freedom from within–by using the method in this little book.

I have gained hope once again after a long, long time, and my *promise* to you is that you too will become hopeful, when you *faithfully* follow the concepts and apply the five-step technique that follows in the NEXT chapter–for the first time, you will be on your way for a life of hope and purpose.

CHAPTER 9

Five Steps to Inner Freedom

Mental reconstruction of our self-talk sounds a sophisticated, complex task. I assure you that it does not have to be the case. Applying the method of this little book is as simple as counting with your five fingers. The main idea of the method is to recognize that Personal Emotional Dependence (our *Oúhou-oúhou*) is rooted in clouded thinking, <u>and</u> learn how to identify what drama script clouded thoughts push us to play. Once we become conscious of the real cause of cloudy thinking <u>and</u> what drama script we are about to play, we can exercise our free will to stop enacting such an unhealthy drama script.

Applying the method of this book is as simple as counting with your five fingers. The main idea of the method is to recognize that Personal Emotional Dependence (our Oúhou-oúhou) is rooted in clouded thinking, <u>and</u> learn how to identify what drama script clouded thoughts push us to play.

By now, you should have become familiar with the following:

a. Your Personal Emotional Dependence (PED).
b. The name/nickname of your Personal Emotional Dependence.
c. The principal drama script you tend to enact in daily life.
d. Cloudy thoughts are generated by our Personal Emotional Dependence (from our personal *Oúhou-oúhou*).

If you have any doubt about the name of your Personal Emotional Dependence (your *Oúhou-oúhou* name), or about detecting your principal drama script, please go back to the previous chapters and reread them carefully again as this chapter builds upon these previous ideas. It is essential to have a crystal-clear understanding of your PED name, what it means to you as well as the principal drama script you tend to be engaged to learn the five-step method in this chapter.

*By following the simple, five-steps that follow, you will be
able to recognize emotionally dependent thoughts easily
and provide the appropriate remedy "on the fly!"*

By following the simple, five-steps that follow, you will be able to recognize emotionally dependent thoughts easily and provide the appropriate remedy "on the fly!" You will learn to correct your self-talk by shifting your thoughts from being negatively charged to being emotionally neutral, and in doing so, setting your little, inner monologue free from *the enslaving power* of Personal Emotional Dependence (your personal *Oúhou-oúhou*).

❧

The Five Steps to Inner Freedom

The five steps that correct our self-talk, setting our little, inner monologue free from emotionally charged thoughts are:

A. Stop and Breathe

It is easy to recognize emotionally dependent thoughts as they give a "gut feeling" that something is wrong; something in our little, self-talk is neither right, nor natural. Once you sense or suspect an emotionally dependent (charged) thought, just stop! Consciously make a pause–take a mental time-out. Just be patient with that thought, with that way of thinking! Resist the temptation to respond with another reactive thought and manner! (That is the reactive nature of your little, inner monologue we aim to correct).

You can make a pause of the stream of thoughts, by saying to yourself, "Wait a minute!" or "just a second!" Take a few deep breaths to release tension. In this way, we do not become reactive to our inner monologue. By reacting too fast, we may take too seriously what our inner speech has to say. Remember, we do not take distorted thoughts seriously or rationally, despite how convincing or dramatic they may appear. Such thoughts may look as if they are realistic, logical and dramatic–do not be deceived, as their purpose is to induce you to engage in one of the three drama scripts! We do not try to face emotionally distorted thoughts with reason–our purpose is to learn how to neutralize them by identifying them and then learn *how to amuse and set them aside.*

B. Reflect, Acknowledge, and Label

Acknowledge that it is your PED responsible for cloudy thinking, and then name that thought with the *name* of your Personal Emotional Dependence.

Tracing the cause of each cloudy thought.

Take time to reflect on that given thought. First, you have to see and recognize your Personal Emotional Dependence as *the root* behind the emotionally-charged thoughts and depressive thinking. Note that your personal emotional dependence is deeply hidden and ingrained in nearly every emotionally distorted thought.

Once you realize that the real cause of the cloudy thinking of the moment is your Personal Emotional Dependence (your personal *Oúhou-oúhou*) then <u>immediately NAME that thought or thinking with your PED name</u>. By doing so, you consciously gain awareness that your cloudy thought is *generated* by your Personal Emotional Dependence (your personal *Oúhou-oúhou*). It is caused by that image, person, relationship, memory, hope, or dream that brings intimacy, deep feelings of affection, romance, and closeness (warmth) of heart. It is anything in life, which could give or could have given meaning to the very existence of your being; nonetheless, life, unfavorable circumstances, and adversities refused to provide for you, or have taken away from you.

Amusing cloudy thoughts one at a time

How do you amuse and set aside such cloudy thoughts? Simply by *labeling* each cloudy thought with your PED name! Imagine each thought carrying a little cloud over it. In fact, each negatively charged thought carries a small 'gray' cloud. By naming (labeling) each dark thought in our little, inner monologue with the *name or nickname* of our Personal Emotional Dependence, we *discharge* the darkness and negativity of that thought's little cloud. As a result, we effectively *unwind* that thought's power over us.

C. Identify Your Drama Script

Identify the type of drama script the clouded thought pushes you to enact.

Once you recognize that it is your Personal Emotional Dependence (your personal *Oúhou-oúhou*) that is responsible for your cloudy, emotionally charged thinking, the next step is to ask yourself what drama script this thinking motivates you to enact? As we have already mentioned, there are three main drama scripts people like to play; therefore, it will be easy for you to decide which one you tend to fall into at any given moment, with any given emotionally-charged thought! If you do not think that thought falls within your principal drama script, then that thought should fall into one of the other two drama scripts. Remember that in the long run we tend to engage in one of the three drama scripts; in the short-term, nevertheless, our little, inner monologue shifts and fluctuates continually among the three principal drama scripts.

So, what are you thinking right now?

So let us get down to the business of examining our way of thinking. What are you thinking right now? How does that thought of yours color your thinking? How does that thought prompt you to react? What type of drama script are you motivated to engage in as your reaction to that thought? Is that thought making you a "Loser," a "Hunter," or a "Narcissist?" Stated in a different way, does that thought make you feel that life has taken away something valuable from you and that you cannot carry on with your life? Or, does that thought induce you to go after an illusion for intimacy? Alternatively, does that thought bring you feelings of pseudo-contentment, indicating that you engage in the Narcissist, "I have-it-all," "Self-absorbed" drama script?

Shifting your self-talk from 'dependence to 'independence mode

When you learn to recognize and name emotionally-charged thoughts (at any given moment) with the NAME of your PED, you are shifting your little, inner self-talk from 'dependence mode' to 'independence mode,' the free thinking that brings clarity to mind. As you learn to neutralize suspected emotionally dependent thoughts by consciously identifying them <u>and then naming them</u>, you neutralize emotional dependence thinking and behavior—and as a result your inner freedom starts to expand day-by-day, thought-by-thought. Once you become *conscious* and identify in what drama script PED (your personal *Oúhou-oúhou*) is causing you to be trapped, in essence *you detach yourself* from the clouded thought, and the power Personal Emotional Dependence has on you—you are set free from the power of your Personal Emotional Dependence!

Cloudy thoughts used to own us

Before learning to recognize your PED (your personal *Oúhou-oúhou*) in your self-talk, emotionally dependent thoughts used to own you–they were part of you–You were part of them–you were emotionally dependent. By learning to carefully identify your PED *as the root* behind each clouded thought, and by understanding what drama script it causes you to play, in essence, *you separate that thought from your being*. That thought is not part of you–you manage to set it aside and thus the harmful potential of that thought is successfully neutralized.

By naming that thought with the name of our Personal Emotional Dependence (our personal *Oúhou-oúhou name*), we *instantly realize* that we are not that thought and that thought is not us. That thought is not part of you any longer, as by identifying and labeling it with the name of your PED (your personal *Oúhou-oúhou* name) you have marginalized it from your little, inner monologue. As a result, that thought ceases to be dangerous, as it is no longer negatively charged. That thought has no power over you to induce you to play out any of the three drama scripts.

D. The Moment of Truth–Your moment of Freedom

Now that you have separated yourself from your Personal Emotional Dependence, and learned to neutralize cloudy thinking by boxing it, labeling it, and setting it aside, you have created a space (inner freedom) between your thought and your next action. You are at last free to decide and take different action than the dramatized behavior of the three drama scripts!

The inner freedom that you create, when you neutralize emotional dependent thinking, increases your freedom of choice and will serve your genuine needs. You will be making choices that come from deep within, from your true, genuine self–from your deepest human needs–from what you really want instead of acting on what your compulsive drama script *dictates*. You will be deciding using your true human attributes that are imagination, conscience, self-awareness, and response-ability (freedom of choice).

Now that you are set free from the three drama scripts, your choices are no longer limited, your inner freedom is without limits, and your life becomes full of unlimited possibilities. You are no longer enslaved by the longings of your childhood. You are no longer enslaved to that person, relationship, memory, hope (true or imaginary) that used to bring you *intimacy*, deep feelings of affection, romance, and closeness (warmth) of heart. You are not *chained* any longer to your past–you are set free from it to face the *present* and you are empowered from within to make sound decisions beyond your false drama script. You are free to take decisions that are in agreement with your true needs that will improve your circumstances right now. Go ahead and make a free choice!

E. Act upon the Moment of Truth

Now is the decisive moment. Now is your chance to take action, to make proactive choices. As long as you keep on separating and detaching distorted thoughts from your little, inner monologue by *amusing them with the NAME of your Personal Emotional Dependence,* you are setting cloudy, depressive thinking aside–you become free to take those decisions that improve your personal circumstances. *Amusing* depressive thoughts with the name of your PED (your personal *Oúhou-oúhou* name) *thought by thought*, you are set free from the yearnings and longings of your childhood, which are hidden behind every negatively charged thought that steals your inner freedom and distorts your self-talk, depriving you of the ability to think and act like a decent human being. *The newly found freedom sets you free from decisions based on unrealistic expectations, longings, wishful thinking, insecurities and fears.*

Taking Action!

By identifying and recognizing, that Personal Emotional Dependence (your personal *Oúhou-oúhou*) is the root behind emotionally charged thoughts, your mind is not emotionally colored by past experiences any longer. This newly-found freedom, nevertheless, demands action on your part. You are free and because you are free, you can act, you can pro-act, and you can make strategic, wise choices based on free will, refusing to act on decisions based on the shortsighted, reactive feelings and attitudes of the enslaving, cloudy thoughts.

☯

Summary of the Five Steps:

To help you *de-dramatize* your thought life, depressive thinking is neutralized by labeling cloudy thoughts with your PED name, and by becoming mindful of what drama script it produces without your will. Once you label each destructive thought with your PED name, you become aware that this thought is not part of you anymore. _The thought has been amused by your PED name and therefore neutralized and set aside_. The drama script you are about to play in response to this type of thinking is an outsider, an intruder! And now it will be your decision, if you want to continue to limit yourself by acting out your old drama script–or to make a choice that will reflect your newly-found freedom, which will serve your needs, and build your own life script that reflects your uniqueness as a human being!

Discharging emotional dependent thoughts takes very little practice, once we have clarified what 'Personal Emotional Dependence' means to us as well as what drama scripts we personally tend to fall into because of PED (because of our personal _Oúhou-oúhou_). By learning and applying the five-steps, I am confident that you will be able to recognize clouded thinking easily, and provide appropriate remedy "on the fly, " _by amusing such thoughts with your PED name_– correcting, therefore, your little, inner monologue.

For the chapters that follow, I will help you _rewrite_ your true Life Script by addressing critical aspects of your humanity such as that of love, your life's mission, and lastly by addressing the spiritual dimension of your human nature.

CHAPTER 10

Rewriting your True Life Script: Rediscovering your Life's Purpose and Mission

Once cloudy thoughts are recognized and amused by naming them, our little, inner monologue brings about a new sense of freedom—our self-talk creates a space for new options and choices that enables us to view the world with a new eye and a clearer perspective, empowering us to live life in a new life script.

In the previous chapter, we have introduced a five-step method, which neutralizes depressive thoughts and *de-clutters* our little, inner monologue on the 'fly,' expanding inner freedom one thought at a time. We have been taught a simple technique of how to *recognize and detach us* from the three enslaving drama scripts that are responsible for burdensome thoughts and feelings. At last, we have a practical tool that sets us free from the *snare* of Personal Emotional Dependence that is hidden behind cloudy thinking, feelings and actions. Once cloudy thoughts are recognized and amused by *naming* them, our little, inner monologue brings about a new sense of freedom–our self-talk creates a *space* for new options and choices that enables us to view the world with a new eye and a clearer perspective, empowering us to live life in a new life script.

In this chapter, we are going to talk about how we can *rewrite* a new healthy script that gives meaning and purpose to life– a life script that will replace the three compulsive drama scripts of the past and will take life in a new direction.

1. You are not on your own: You were born with a mission

As I have already mentioned in previous chapters, contrary to what you were told, or have believed–you do not own life and life does not owe you–you *owe everything* to life! Said differently, your happiness, lasting peace and fulfillment depends on how well you discover who you actually are, and how well *you can make a difference in this world*, using the rare talents and gifts life has bestowed on you from birth.

Again, I would like to emphasize this simple life principle: _The truth about you is that you are not here by accident._ You are here for a reason. You were born with a *purpose* and a mission to fulfill. You have a *rare uniqueness* that no one else in the world has. Therefore, you can contribute to the world the way no one else can! You have a uniqueness, which is *crying out* to be lived. Despite your daily difficulties and tragedies, or how people have treated you, life needs you–the world needs you. A mission awaits you on this planet that *only you* can accomplish! Despite what your imperfect self-talk or what your critical, little monologue may whisper, you can find happiness and lasting peace *by finding* your unique place in life.

> *"We didn't give ourselves the personalities, talents,*
> *or longings–we were born with them. When we fulfill*
> *these–these gifts from beyond ourselves–it is like fulfilling*
> *something we were meant to do.*[21]*"*
> Michael Novak, author of *"Business as a Calling."*

2. Looking outside for an inside matter:
Be cautious of the Sophists of Today.

It was the Sophists who first taught courses to the Athenians and other Greek cities since more than 2,500 years ago that *resemble so much* our modern "quick success" schemes and "happiness now!" seminars.

For finding success in life, in essence, the ancient as well as the modern *sophists* advocate that *you can be anything you want to be* in life, if you work hard enough. All it takes is knowledge and effort, they claim. In other words, for the modern sophists of our culture, personal predisposition and inborn qualities are not so important. You can copy others and others can copy you. Career success is just having goals and reaching to achieve these goals. To paraphrase furthermore, according to the modern sophists, everything is relative and you can master any job any skill. When you learn the secret how others did it better, you can do it too– by discovering the shortcuts that others used to achieve success.

You are not just another human clone

In essence, the sophists are still whispering to us absolute pragmatism: Human beings are not necessarily unique individuals with predisposed talents and life calling. The new Sophists insist that We are all created 'equal,' claiming that we have just intelligence and free will–and by combining the two we can do just about *anything* and become just about *anybody*. Said differently, they claim that you and I are just *human clones* and the best way to be successful is to learn to copy each other to increase our knowledge in subjects where we want to succeed.

The popular culture of our times have conditioned us to look outside of us for success, while true success and self-fulfillment starts by learning to build on what we have already stored in our hearts and minds from birth. When we tap into those personal, unique resources, we begin to understand *who we are*, and *what our purpose in life is.*

Looking Outside for an Inside matter

You and I have been trained to look *outside ourselves* for success, although success is an "inside-out" matter. The "outside-in" approach to fulfillment, unfortunately, is causing a distorted, unreal, little, inner monologue, in which the results and consequences have been *devastating* for our emotional health, self-respect, and human dignity: The "outside-in" approach, in essence, ensures that we compulsively adopt and blindly engage in one of the three drama scripts–with tragic consequences on our emotional well-being and life potential.

Nonetheless, you *cannot* attain success when you copy and when you imitate the success of others! Success is an "inside" job and you become successful when you recognize, nourish, and use you *rare* talents and predispositions–*despite how few they may seem.* As long as we continue to play someone else's drama script, we cannot follow our heart and discover our life's calling on planet Earth. On the other hand, when you habitually amuse and neutralize monster little thoughts, day-by-day, your inner freedom expands and empowers you to discover and carry on with your mission to fulfill your life's calling.

"Your time is limited, so don't waste it living someone else's life. Don't be trapped by dogma–which is living with the results of other people's thinking. Don't let the noise of other's opinions drown out your own inner voice. And most important, have the courage to follow your heart and intuition. They somehow already know what you truly want to become. Everything else is secondary"[22].

Commencement address at Stanford University by Steve Jobs, on June 12, 2005

3. Your Personal Ithaca–The road to reaching your life's calling.

As Konstantinos Kavafis[23] has described it in his poem *"Ithaca,"* your Ithaca is the road to your destination–your life's calling. Ithaca consists of the unique and special talents only you possess to make a distinct contribution in this world and the generations to come. Your Ithaca is your road to *realizing your uniqueness and calling in life* to serve humanity, because serving humanity is synonymous to serving your deepest needs.

Here is Kavafis' famous poem in its entirety:

ITHACA[24]
As you set out for Ithaca
hope your road is a long one,
full of adventure, full of discovery.
Laistrygonians, Cyclops,
angry Poseidon–don't be afraid of them:
you'll never find things like that one on your way
as long as you keep your thoughts raised high,
as long as a rare excitement
stirs your spirit and your body.
Laistrygonians, Cyclops,
wild Poseidon–you won't encounter them
unless you bring them along inside your soul,
unless your soul sets them up in front of you.

Hope your road is a long one.
May there be many summer mornings when,
with what pleasure, what joy,
you enter harbours you're seeing for the first time;

may you stop at Phoenician trading stations
to buy fine things, mother of pearl and coral, amber and ebony,
sensual perfumes of every kind—
as many sensual perfumes as you can;
and may you visit many Egyptian cities
to learn and go on learning from their scholars.

Keep Ithaca always in your mind.
Arriving there is what you're destined for.
But don't hurry the journey at all.
Better if it lasts for years,
so you're old by the time you reach the island,
wealthy with all you've gained on the way,
not expecting Ithaca to make you rich.

Ithaca gave you the marvellous journey.
Without her you wouldn't have set out.
She has nothing left to give you now.

And if you find her poor, Ithaca won't have fooled you.
Wise as you will have become, so full of experience,
you'll have understood by then what these Ithacas mean

Constantine P. Cavafy.

Your Ithaca: A step-by-step explanation

Explanation of the poem "Ithaca":

Constantine P. Cavafy enjoys a reputation as one of the finest Greek poets. *"Ithaca"* is one of his internationally best-known poems and is considered to express the outlook of free, inner living, by adopting a dependence-free inner monologue to respond to life's challenges and follow *our life's* true mission and calling.

Poem Introduction:

"Ithaca" is an unrhymed poem of five stanzas that employ conversational, everyday language. The narrator (probably a man who has travelled a lot) addresses Odysseus, the hero of Homer's epic poem *"The Odyssey."* The poet tells us that what is important is not Ithaca, the island home that was the goal of Odysseus's years of wandering–but wisdom, character, knowledge, and experience gained from the journey.

A modern paraphrase would have been that "real success is *change in character*–the experience, knowledge, and wisdom gained while reaching our life's calling–a goal which benefits are greater than the goal itself." Conclusively, Success as we know it, is the *by-product* of character development than the end itself.

Your road to Ithaca–your journey:

Ithaca is the personal journey every one of us has to travel in response to the talents and gifts life has bestowed on us. Once we become aware and acknowledge our unique mission and life's calling, the main obstacles to reaching our destination will not be coming so much from outer circumstances of life's journey as much as they will come from our Personal Emotional Dependence, our distorted self-talk, our short sighted, little, inner monologue.

What the poem actually says is that we have to *respond* to our life's true calling giving the best of us without worrying so much for success and for the respective rewards and benefits. Success within its modern definition is the result of character building–not the end and focus of your mission. Character comes before success as the development of character experience, knowledge, and wisdom gained while aiming at something higher than yourself is more valuable than the rewards of success.

> " . . . *Laistrygonians, Cyclops,*
> *angry Poseidon–don't be afraid of them:*
> *you'll never find things like that one on your way*
> *as long as you keep your thoughts raised high . . ."*

The Laistrygonians, Cyclops, and the wild Poseidon–we will not encounter unless we carry them along in our soul, unless we allow them to *dominate* our inner, little monologue and self-talk. In other words, the mythical monsters, the Laistrygonians and the Cyclops *reside in* your inner, little thinking, and attempt to make you a slave to your Personal Emotional Dependence (your personal *Oúhou-oúhou*). Such mythical monsters are emotional strongholds, the *changing faces* of your Personal Emotional Dependence, which if you listen and act on them by the means of the three enslaving drama scripts, *you will be led astray*, away from your life's true destination–away from your *true calling* and true living–away from your *Ithaca*.

Furthermore, we emphasize that it is not so much the adverse conditions in our life's journey that cause problems. The real enemy and the war takes place *within us*–it is the tendency of the mind to create mythical monsters in our little, inner self-talk. The angry Poseidon the Laistrygonians, and Cyclops, in everyday living, are monster, little thoughts generated by our Personal Emotional Dependence (our personal *Oúhou-oúhou*). It is by your Personal Emotional Dependence you are at war with–not so much with the difficulties of life. The bad circumstances serve as *triggers*, which trigger inadequacies and unsettled, emotional dependences in us–that's all they are! It is up to us to learn to neutralize such burdening little, thoughts and thus creating the necessary space and freedom that would further develop our inner freedom to follow our mission and reach our destination–our Ithaca!

Do not be afraid of what life throws at you; instead, build the habit of *"keeping your thoughts raised high,"* by maintaining the right attitude, which comes from your identity as a member of the human race. Such dependence-free thinking will keep your liberated from the inner Laistrygonians and Cyclops, and any other *forms* of little, cloudy thoughts, created by your Personal Emotional Dependence (your personal *Oúhou-oúhou*).

> *"Hope your road is a long one.*
> *May there be many summer mornings when,*
> *with what pleasure, what joy,*

you enter harbours you're seeing for the first time;
may you stop at Phoenician trading stations
to buy fine things,
mother of pearl and coral, amber and ebony,
sensual perfumes of every kind—
as many sensual perfumes as you can;
and may you visit many Egyptian cities
to learn and go on learning from their scholars. "

"Keep Ithaca always in your mind.
Arriving there is what you're destined for.
But don't hurry the journey at all.
Better if it lasts for years . . ."

Explanation:

There is no hurry on your way to your Ithaca–take your time while travelling and approach your journey with plea-sure, joy, expectation and excitement. Nevertheless, *keep Ithaca always in your mind.*

In your road to meet your destiny, avoid false hopes for *shortcuts*, as they are none! Fulfilling your life's calling takes a lifetime of effort, commitment and principle-based living. Take all the time you can for regular breaks and self-renewal that will empower you to travel and enjoy the journey of your mission–nevertheless, keep Ithaca always in your little, thoughts. Ithaca is your unique destination, your life's call-ing, your destiny–your very self.

"And if you find her poor, Ithaca won't have fooled you.
Wise as you will have become, so full of experience, you'll
have understood by then what these Ithacas mean."

It's easy to allow our little *self-talk* to enter into *illusory* drama scripts by desiring what the world wants, looking for an outside source of fulfillment–when true fulfillment *lies in us* (in our calling). You are not to allow yourself to experience disappointment when your mission seems poor in the world's eyes. Avoid the temptation to compare the world's definition of happiness as true success is *accepting yourself* for what you are, and by responding to your life's calling, *despite how humble and poor your mission may seem in the world's eyes*. Experience the joy of freedom that springs out of the knowledge that you live a life with the mission set just for you.

Challenge your self-talk by asking these important questions of yourself:

What if your life's calling is to be an extraordinary mother or father, when the world entices you to climb the corporate ladder? In the world's view, the worth of your mission may be of trivial value, but in the minds of the children whom you will make a difference, there is no monetary value you can attach to it–it is beyond any monetary worth and material reward to be able to make a difference in other human beings!

Conclusion

To *rewrite* your life script, you have to learn who you are–the unique talents and skills you have–and to *discover and follow* your life's calling. On your road to Ithaca, Cyclops and the Laistrygonians you will not encounter–when you learn to set your mind above your circumstances.

The Cyclopes and the Laistrygonians are monster thoughts that are created in our inner thinking when we *choose* to accept and act on such cloudy thoughts. Instead, learn to recognize your *principal drama script* behind those mythical monsters–*amuse* those little, monster thoughts with the *name* of your Personal Emotional Dependence (you personal *Oúhou-oúhou* name) and shift your mind–in this manner–to inner freedom, that will reassure your *true mission* and road to your final destination–your road to Ithaca.

CHAPTER 11

Rewriting your True Life Script:
The Three Drama Scripts . . . in love

In the last chapter, we have talked about how we find meaning and purpose in life, and how the elusive Personal Emotional Dependence manifests in our little, inner monologue as monster thoughts to obstruct us from traveling the road to destination. In this and the following chapter, we will talk about another important aspect of human existence–the mystery and paradox of Love. On one hand, if properly understood and nurtured, the "love" dimension of our humanity has the potential to bring immense happiness, joy, and peace. On the other hand, love can be a source of suffering and misery–when we fail to understand *love* thoroughly. In this chapter, we will describe the three drama scripts we like to play . . . in love, while on the next chapter, we will *redefine love* and set the role of feelings into a new perspective.

On Eros, Love, and Personal Emotional Dependence: Can you tell the difference?

The modern culture of today–with its subjective value system–have trained our minds to believe in a set of confusing definitions of the *nature* of love. Today, there are indeed a set of overwhelmingly confusing meanings for what true love, erotic passion, and physical intimacy mean. As a result, today's media *use* the above words in an interchanging, vague, and obscure manner–bringing *uncertainty* to our thinking and little, inner self-talk.

The Misleading Definition of Love

Ultimately, there is no area in our lives in which Personal Emotional Dependence (our personal *Oúhou-oúhou*) can be so misleading and deceptive as in the area of erotic passion and love. A person's distorted little, inner monologue, acutely deprived of genuine love, will search and pursue 'love' more intensely than for any other human need.

The difference between Personal Emotional Dependence (Our personal Oúhou-oúhou–a utopian need which was formed and crystallized in a person's heart during childhood) <u>and</u> genuine, love–the type of love which should set us free– is blurred to a dangerous degree!

The blurred understanding of love and its imminent dangers

For the starving, emotionally deprived persons, genuine love and PED are the same: Both genuine love *and* a person's Personal Emotional Dependence, smell, look and feel *alike*. With no real ability to distinguish between the two on the conscious level, people tend to attach to them the same definition and meaning. The difference between Personal Emotional Dependence (Our personal *Oúhou-oúhou*–a utopian need which was formed and crystallized in a person's heart during childhood) <u>and</u> genuine, love–the type of love which should set us free–is *blurred* to a dangerous degree!

How do people pursue love?

In daily life, people (subconsciously) chase for a partner who will satisfy the void in their heart, the void created by Personal Emotional Dependence. People expect to find in their partner *that image, person, relationship, memory, hope, or dream that will bring intimacy, deep feelings of affection, romance, and closeness of heart.* In essence, people *do not* pursue genuine love, but an *unmet need* created by their Personal Emotional Dependence (their personal *Oúhou-oúhou*).

> *In essence, people do not pursue genuine love, but an unmet need created by their Personal Emotional Dependence (their personal Oúhou-oúhou).*

Recognizing your principal love drama script

The ability to *recognize* Personal Emotional Dependence and the principal drama script that is operating in our relationships will give us the freedom to either walk away, or stay in the relationship and work at it with our partner–until we nurture it enough to mature and set free from the traps of Personal Emotional Dependence.

Before explaining in detail how each drama script is manifested in love relations, let us briefly review the characteristics of each drama script. The first drama (The 'Loser' drama script) describes people who have lost something valuable that they were not entitled to have; the second drama (the 'Hunter' drama script) describes individuals who pursue and chase something valuable they will never get. Likewise, the third, the "Narcissist," Self-absorbed drama script describes persons who think they got it all in life.

Although there are significant differences among the three main drama scripts, all the three drama scripts *portray* a dependent personality–a person who is at *high risk* of clinical depression. What the three drama scripts have in common is that they *ensnare* people in a drama with their *misleading Personal Emotional Dependence*. People acting the first drama script experience a final, irreversible deprivation of their utopian PED. The second drama script portrays people who are searching for an *illusion* to fill the void of their PED while the third drama script describes people who *live an illusion*–narcissistic individuals who falsely believe that they have found their PED (their personal Ohou-ouhou).

First drama play:
The Loser drama script . . . in love

Like little children, people in the 'Loser' drama wait for others to satisfy their emotional needs. They desire to be loved, but they do not realize that love must be nurtured from their side as well in order for it to grow.

As we have described previously, the 'Loser' drama script is enacted by persons who exhibit a "they-took-it-from-me" negative attitude–believing that life and circumstances took from them all hope for happiness and fulfillment. In the mind of such people, their expectations to fulfill their PED (*. . . that something that would have brought deep feelings of affection, romance, closeness of heart, and meaning to the very existence of their being . . .)* is lost forever–without the slightest chance of recovery.

As a result, such deprived, negative attitude is deeply rooted in their personalities, emotions, and conduct. People trapped in the 'Loser' drama, blame others and life for their perceived unfavorable circumstances, inadequacies and hopelessness. They have a strong tendency to think that life *owes* them something that could have made them fulfilled and satisfied. *'It was life's responsibility to give to them what they wanted,'* they believe, although in reality, they blame life for something they never had, or they were *never entitled* to own.

When persons trapped in the 'Loser' drama script enter into a love relationship, they do not believe their relationship has any room for improvement. In their mind, all hope for love (and life) is lost–so it is for their relationship.

Respectively, they go with the "as good as it gets" attitude, characterized by *apathy* and relationship *stagnation*. Like little children, people in the 'Loser' drama wait for others to satisfy their emotional needs. They desire to be loved, but they do not realize that love must be nurtured from *their side* as well in order for it to grow. Although life may have given them a good partner, such individuals are not content with their partner, nor do they care to make any positive contribution that would improve their relationship.

It is worth mentioning that in *extreme cases,* people trapped in the 'Loser' love drama script *blame* their partner for every little fault with an "It's always your fault," attitude. It is the fault of *the other* partner–never their fault. They continue to accuse their partner, making the other partner feel guilty for the condition of their relationship, thus killing the other partner's dignity and self-confidence.

In such extreme cases of the 'Loser' drama script–be warned! You as a partner may be a good husband or wife who wants your relationship to grow with your other half. Nevertheless, your partner's 'Loser' attitude can be *self-destructive*. Persons who engage in the 'Loser' drama script tend to make their partner feel stuck–trapped–in the relationship. While their partner is doing everything possible to improve the relationship, not only they stay uninvolved, but they also *dampen* any positive changes for improvement.

Suggested remedy for you or your partner:
If you realize that *you or your partner* is frequently *entangled* in the 'Loser' drama script, the first step is to rectify the value system of your little, inner monologue, by *rereading* the chapters "on Truth" , "on You" , "on Life" because the

principal reasons for the enactment of the 'Loser' drama script are _unrealistic assumptions_ and _faulty expectations about life_. The chapter on discovering and _naming_ your or your partner's Personal Emotional Dependence is also recommended. In addition, learning to apply the five-steps to inner freedom will create enough _inner freedom_ that will gradually bring positive results in your relationship.

Second, I strongly recommend for you or your partner to discover your "life's calling," the activity that will make you or your partner "tick" again. Such a discovery does not have to require career change or any other significant change in your life. Self-discovery is a gradual process; it can start with finding a fulfilling hobby, involvement in community work–any activity that can inject _hope and zest_ in life once again. Life may have not been so generous by giving you as many talents as others have–nevertheless; life gave _at least one talent_ to every one of us. The key is for you or your partner to discover this _single talent_, nourish it, and start building on it. Such a self-discovery will considerably improve your or your partner's self-esteem and _inner freedom_, which in turn will make a _positive contribution_ on your relationship with your partner.

Second script:
The 'Hunter' drama script . . . in love.

People trapped in the 'Hunter' drama look for the *ideal relationship*. In their subconscious quest for idealized intimacy, such persons seek after the *ultimate partner*, a partner who will satisfy their needs for affection, romance, and the so many other utopian needs they crave for–the partner who will make them completely happy and *fulfilled*.

Back in the mind of such individuals, their little, inner voice will continue to compare their partner <u>with</u> PED (their personal Oúhou-oúhou)–comparing their partner with a utopia, an idealized person–and his or her partner will always fall short in such comparison.

Attracted by Physical or Outer Appearances

People trapped in the "Hunter" drama script focus on the physical, external appearance of their partner–such as physical attractiveness, career, social status, and financial standing. When 'Hunters' look in the eyes of a potential partner, good character, compatibility, ability to communicate and other *personal virtues* (that are essential for successful relationship) do not get their attention.

Daily conduct of lovers living in the 'Hunter' drama script

In a relation, lovers who engage in the 'Hunter' drama script, set *high expectations* for their partner, while they do not know how to build a relationship themselves. Yes, they may work hard and make anything possible to satisfy their partner's material needs–yet, they fail to *understand and connect* with their partner! By focusing on physical attractiveness, social status, career, and financial standing, lovers entangled in the 'Hunter' drama script are unaware of the *fundamentals* of how a relationship can grow and succeed. The sad phenomenon with the Hunter drama script is that they may find a partner who has the right chemistry, the right compatibility–a person in other words with whom there are foundations for a fulfilling relationship. Nevertheless, the relationship will be destined to doom, as these persons are *rarely satisfied* with their partner. Back in the mind of such individuals, their little, inner voice will continue to compare their partner <u>with</u> PED (their personal *Oúhou-oúhou*)–*comparing their partner with a utopia, an idealized person*–and his or her partner will always *fall short* in such comparison.

Because life and people are less than ideal, and perfect circumstances seldom exist, Hunters *get easily disappointed* with their current partner and give up on their relationship too easily. As their current partner does not meet their *unrealistic expectations*, Hunters tend to move from relationship to relationship, thinking and hoping that the *next partner* will be the right one–the one who will bring fulfillment, love, and contentment.

Always on the move, *questing* for the perfect woman or the perfect man, lovers trapped in the 'Hunter' drama script are after an *illusion*–they are looking for an ideal person who does not exist in real life! In their quest for Mr. or Mrs. Perfect, the real drama of lovers *entangled* in this script, is that they are trapped in a *vicious circle*, moving from partner to partner, from relationship to relationship without a happy ending–with limited possibility to experience love and fulfillment.

Remedy for lovers trapped in the 'Hunter' drama script

As the central feature of this drama script is *'lack of contentment,'* persons easily entangled in the 'hunter' drama script must learn to gain satisfaction from life, not just by 'doing,' but also by 'being.' Hunters need to learn how to *relax their expectations* and start enjoying the world around them–including their partner! In addition, they need to view their partner and their relationship not just from the outer point of view but from the inside as well. Beauty, social status, and financial standing may be important to look for in a man or in a woman; nevertheless, *character* is often more valuable as it is more *enduring* for the challenges of life. Instead of hunting for glamorous characteristics in a partner, hunters ought to also search for virtues such as honesty, faithfulness, simplicity, and ability to connect. Individuals easily entangled in this drama script should include *a list of internal virtues,* along with their favorite external attributes in their quest for a suitable partner.

Once they are involved in a relationship, Hunters ought to learn how to take a break and *invest* in their relationship by spending quality time with their partner. As the tendency of the 'Hunter' drama script is to move from project to project, from goal to goal, many times Hunters must be *forced* by their partner to take regular breaks, avoid working during weekends, and arrange time to be with their partner. I would recommend setting appointed 'dates' in which they and their partner meet and spend time in places other than home or business. By creating "time spaces," both partners will have the chance to connect and refill each other's emotional bank account. By spending quality leisure time together with mutual friends, or in nature, will soften their hunter drama tendencies, and will help hunters behave more sociably, more humanely, with more understanding toward their partner.

Third drama script: The Narcissist . . . in love

To refresh our memory, let us summarize the third drama script. People *entangled* in the "Narcissist" drama script are sometimes successful people, or people who seem to have "made it" in life. In many occasions, they are persons whom talents society esteems the most. They are characterized with high intelligence in the field of science, business, or the arts. Unfortunately, in the end their *expertise* becomes their god–the only life aspect they value . . . and worship! They are dragged in by their passion, which consumes and blinds them to the other important roles they also have to live in life. As I have mentioned in the previous chapters, persons who enact the Narcissistic drama script are so good at what they do that eventually they are consumed by it. Their "highly-in-demand" talent, craft, or expertise becomes the center of interest, focus, and attention. The other important roles in life *orbit around* their passion just as planets orbit around the sun–*with lower priority and significance.*

Their partner is just another tool whom they need to facilitate their pursuit of their passion. Their partner fits their agenda, their plan! For such narcissists, their "other half" is just a pleasant accessory that complements their self-absorbed, self-consumed way of life.

Such self-complacent persons have a self-generated sense of self-importance, which is often given to them by popular culture, placing themselves at the *center* of their own little world. For such individuals, their partner is . . . an object. Their partner is just *another tool* whom they need to facilitate their pursuit of their passion. Their partner fits their agenda, their plan! For such *narcissists*, their "other half" is just a pleasant accessory that complements their self-absorbed, self-consumed way of life. Although such individuals may be good persons, they are *unaware* of their self-absorption, and they lack understanding of other *principal roles* life is calling them to play. As Narcissists are consumed by their passion, little by little the other aspects of their life are fading away–including the relationship with their lover. They just care how best to act out their emotional drama script–their agenda, their hobby, their career passion, their idolized expertise, rather than *contributing and nurturing* an equally important dimension of their life–their intimate relation with their partner.

As I have mentioned in the past, "Narcissist" is the most tragic drama script, as the pseudo-complacence people experience from deeply pursuing their passion does not allow them to sense any empathy with their partner's feelings and communication needs. They may even love their partner, but still they need to feel the pain of *separation or loss* to realize it.

Who gets depressed in this drama script?

The partner of the "Narcissist" is usually the candidate for clinical depression, because their partners receive little or no love and attention. On the other side of the relationship, individuals entangled in this drama script are serious candidates for severe depression–even suicide, when their trait ceases to attract interest and esteem from business or from the ever-changing modern culture. When the demand for their high level of expertise fades or dies, *they die with it as well.*

Suggested remedy for the "Narcissist" . . . in love:

As we have mentioned, in the beginning, the person who is entangled in this drama script must experience a *catastrophe or a great loss* to wake up from his or her illusionary, little world. In terms of what their partner is supposed to do in this dead-end relationship, there are no easy answers–only radical actions and solutions–which you must take to wake up your partner and drag them back into the real world. I can assure you that by doing nothing to revitalize your relationship–your partner will keep on treating you as an accessory, treating you as an object, whom s/he needs–to live out their passion–be it career, hobby, relation, or any other activity!

For the Narcissist, your presence is a necessity, who they must have in order to pursue their passion–and continue to *sink in* their pseudo-content drama script and self-consuming, little golden cage. By taking action now, you will save your partner from greater trouble later–when their pursuits will not be "in fashion" anymore–when their passion will no longer be in demand by the changing tastes of popular culture.

The "Narcissist" Love Drama Script: The other side of the coin

It would be a great omission not to mention the other side of the "Narcissist" drama script, which is enacted out mostly by women–although I have observed through the years that more men are now trapped into this drama script as well. People in this drama script seems to have a prolonged infatuation with their partner. It is surely not the erotic type of feeling, the initial excitement and infatuation that are present in the first stage of a relationship. Yet, it is a persistent pattern in the relationship that continues even after that first "infatuation" stage, for it has a *dominant* and consistent presence.

Women entangled in this drama script think that the idealized intimacy they are seeking can only be found in their relationship, in their partner–in their man! Having been conditioned by society's false definition of love, women in this drama script make their man an object of worship, an admiration, their god!

Engaging in the "Narcissist" drama script, women tend to think that the idealized intimacy they are seeking, that thing which will deeply satisfy their *great need* for affection, romance, and warmth of heart can only be found in their relationship, in their partner–in their man! Having been conditioned by society's *false* definition of love, which promotes the belief that their partner should be "everything" to them–women in this drama script, make their man an object of worship, an admiration, their god!

Their little, inner monologue whispers, *"I have found him at last. I will do everything to keep him. He is mine! He is the only one who can provide happiness and fulfillment to me . . ."* Unfortunately, such women are unaware that their relationship takes a *controlling direction.* It is the void of their PED (their Personal *Oúhou-oúhou*)–they try to satisfy–as their drama script serves neither the interest of their partner, nor the interest of the relationship.

Characteristics of this love drama script

In response to her false definition of what love is, she compulsively becomes her man's baby-sitter, assumes the role of a mother, a sister, and . . . a slave.

The woman thinks that her man is the *source of meaning* for her emotional existence, and given this assumption, she will sacrifice and do *anything* to keep him. As a result, a possessive, controlling type of unhealthy love is manifested in her, indicating her extreme emotional dependence in her partner. In response to her *false definition* of what love is, she *compulsively* becomes his baby-sitter, assumes the role of a mother, a sister, and . . . a slave. In doing so, she does not know that the magic in the relationship will evaporate and the mystery of love will be easily lost. The man, feeling *suffocated* by her over affection, starts to lose interest in her–or takes her love for granted! On the other hand, because of giving so much to their man, women trapped in this drama script end up feeling *empty*–their self-esteem and dignity are depleted.

In this drama script, Personal Emotional Dependence is mistaken for true love as true love many times may be characterized by suffering for a higher purpose. Said in different way, the hunger to satisfy the PED in these women is mistaken for love. The key idea to remember here is the *low level* of self-esteem, self-respect, and dignity of the woman. Indeed, suffering is sometimes part of everyday reality–even in the most nurtured relationships. Nevertheless, if the woman's self-esteem plummets heavily downward, as she tries to avoid rejection or abandonment from her man, losing her self-respect and human dignity along the way–then it is her Personal Emotional Dependence (her personal *Oúhou-oúhou*) she is serving, not the true interest of her man.

In extreme cases of this drama script, the woman may voluntarily endure verbal or even physical abuse by her partner. Just to keep him, *to continue to be the major player in this drama script*–she rationalizes abuse! Nevertheless, as the time goes by, the confusion between her needy PED (her personal Ouhou-ouhou) and true love opens the door for *further abuse* and human degradation, forming an unending, vicious, and sometimes dangerous cycle.

Even if there is love in her relationship, nevertheless, such relationship can be irreversibly damaged, if the woman does not discover and become conscious that <u>she is too dependent on her man</u>–as well as the reason why she acts in this way. In this case, the problem is not that her man does not love her, but it is because the woman suffers from a needy Personal Emotional Dependence (needy personal Oúhou-oúhou), and therefore *she does not love herself enough!* The woman's heart in this drama script functions like an emotional container that is completely empty, and she is desperately dependent on her man to fill her up and satisfy all her emotional needs–constantly.

Suggested remedy for women entangled in this drama play:

First, the female soul entangled in this drama script needs to become aware and identify her own 'Personal Emotional Dependence' and discover how her unique PED (her personal *Oúhou-oúhou*) traps her in this unhealthy drama script scenario. Recognizing her own drama script will be the first step to her recovery–and to rebalancing her relationship.

Replacing myths, misconceptions with truth

Conditioned by popular culture, many women have been raised to believe that love is a basic human need, just as food and shelter. Nevertheless, love is not a need–*it's a spontaneous choice coming from inner freedom.* The ability to give and receive love comes from inner freedom, when our little, inner monologue is unclogged and set free from the three principal drama scripts we compulsively play to satisfy the void in our Personal Emotional Dependence. True love can never be attained through the compulsive drama script we enact to gain love–no matter what effort or sacrifice we make.

Unconditional love comes from our emotionally *independent* little, inner monologue. It is a product and expression of our true self and not the result of the three drama scripts– or even our good intentions. It is an expression that comes after *we have set ourselves free* from the traps of Personal Emotional Dependence (our personal *Oúhou-oúhou*)–when we learn daily to identify, separate it and send it in the back of our mind. As we *amuse and set aside* Personal Emotional Dependence (our personal *Oúhou-oúhou*), any expression to love or reject, to give or take, comes from our true self, and such choices are genuine and nurturing, as they are not induced by Personal, Emotional Dependence—they come from our real self, our unique character and deepest needs.

The female soul, once she learns to mentally set her little, inner monologue free from the traps of her Personal, Emotional Dependence, she will start to give and receive love *because* of her inner freedom and free choice—as an expression of her unique self. It will be the kind of love that is derived from her true *female identity,* her womanhood, and as a result, love will be lasting and fulfilling.

First, we have to clarify and straighten the woman's little, inner monologue by establishing *principle-based* beliefs on her unique human identity, and *relearn* how to love others. Building new principle-based *beliefs* is essential for her to start experiencing inner freedom. To clarify my position from any possible misunderstanding, there is nothing wrong in being emotionally involved with our partner as long as our spontaneous love does not become over affectionate and over dependent, endangering our self-respect, dignity, and inner freedom.

Creating Space for both partners

Once the *realization* of what her Personal Emotional Dependence is and what drama script she engages in become apparent to her, she first must learn ways to *create space* for her partner who probably feels *asphyxiated* from too much love and all the care he already receives. She also ought to learn to create space for her self by becoming conscious of the *independent side* of her relationship. Whether by experimenting with new activities, exploring her talents and adopting new hobbies, the discovery of *new aspects* of her personality she never knew existed before–all of these will gradually start to create space, her own space that she needs to experience contentment and inner freedom *in herself*. By learning the *independent side* of her relation, it will become apparent to her that it is *the inner freedom in her*, which will allow her to make spontaneous, genuine love contributions contributing to a warmer and more genuine relationship, as a result.

Conclusion

Relationships can be a source of suffering and misery, when we fail to understand *how to relate* with our partners. On the other hand, the "love" dimension in human nature can bring immense happiness, joy, maturity, and peace, when partners learn to identify and set aside the three principal drama scripts they *wrongly enact* to fill the emptiness in their Personal Emotional Dependence. In this chapter we have described the three drama scripts we like to play . . . in love, while on the next chapter, we will *redefine love* and set the role of feelings into a new perspective.

CHAPTER 12

Rewriting your True Life Script: Redefining Love and Putting Feelings in new perspective

What is true love?

In defining true love, we have so far explained what love is not! True love is absent, when we are enslaved and playing out the three drama scripts in our relationships, when we are at the mercy of Personal Emotional Dependence (our personal *Oúhou-oúhou*). Therefore, true love happens when lovers have learned to set aside their Personal Emotional Dependence–when the couple consciously choose not to enact on the three principal drama scripts PED creates.

Regardless, of how we define love, you may agree that true love comes without requirements. Love is unconditional; otherwise, love would have been just another commercial transaction–a give-and-take agreement–just as stocks and bonds are traded in New York's financial markets. On the contrary, love results from a state of heart that *carries* no preconditions and requirements. To be *real*, love must be unconditional–love happens when the couple set aside PED (their personal *Oúhou-oúhou*) and enough inner space is created in their hearts to allow them to make spontaneous, positive choices based on their joint wants and needs. In other words, love becomes real when it is unconditional–when we are free to choose to give, when we are free to choose to love, and when we make these decisions spontaneously with no expectations, or gains–we choose to love simply because we want to make our partner happy as this gives us true joy. Said differently, true love is not the emotional response of a cloudy little, inner self-talk, as true love liberates partners in a relationship–it does not enslave lovers in a drama script–it sets people free. Authentic love is a healthful expression coming from an emotionally independent state of heart–it is the product of a free state of mind, which comes spontaneously from ourselves, from our true wants and deepest needs.

Unconditional love

Unconditional love emerges, when the couple set aside PED (their personal Oúhou-oúhou) and enough inner space is created in their hearts to allow spontaneous, positive choices based on their joint needs and wants.

The Three Stages of Love

Just as Eskimos have about thirty words for the word "snow," in a similar way, the Greek language has three words or more for the word 'love': *Eros*[25], *Philia*[26], and *Agape* love. *Eros* is the type of love based on physical characteristics; *Philia* implies the brotherhood type of love, while *agape* love is the unconditional love, love without strings. Although different from the other, the three types of love are the three stages that lead to love that is emotionally free, when the lovers reach the stage of 'agape' love. Instead of approaching 'eros,' 'philia,' and 'agape' love as mutually exclusive, a better way to view them is in stages, or in terms of a gradual process, which a couple progresses from one stage to the next, moving from an emotional dependent love to unconditional, 'agape' love–love without strings, a lasting love, the union of hearts and minds.

Eros and Philia stages

The term *'Eros '*as you already know, refers to that part of love that is characterized by passionate, intense desire in a relationship. *Eros*, romance, infatuation, and "love at the first sight" are not necessarily without their merits. Romantic love can lead to the next stage of love, when the relationship is properly understood and nurtured–the stage of 'Philia' love.

As partners learn to avoid enacting the three drama scripts and follow their *own*, genuine script, *'Philia'* sets the next stage of their relationship. Within the 'Philia' stage, the couple learns to grow and set aside and respect their differences and become friends. Conflict may exist, but now it is more like a *friendly game* than strife or struggle with each other. Lovers adapt to each other's physical and emotional needs, balance their work and social aspirations and develop new 'joint' friendship as a couple confident of themselves.

Agape love: The ultimate of love

The third type of love or the last, most important stage of the loving process is 'agape' love–and it is the *highest form* of love! It is a selfless love as the partners are almost *free* from PED (free from their personal *Oúhou-oúhou*). Agape is the type of love in which the little, inner monologues of the couple have matured. The couples are characterized by little, inner monologues that have learned to avoid the traps of the three enslaving drama scripts–by systematically setting aside their PED (their personal *Oúhou-oúhou*) out of their thinking, and by creating new little, inner monologues that they share, looking optimistically to a joint future with broad horizons.

Agape love, or unconditional love, is the highest form of love between two human beings–it is the love that accepts each other for who they are, not for what they should be or how well they satisfy each other's expectations. In this stage of love, emotional dependences that used to interfere in the previous love stages are minimized. Agape love is love in which the inner monologue is free from cloudy thoughts generated by the couple's Personal Emotional Dependence that leads to narcissism, envy, anger, egotism, impatience, and unforgiveness. And because agape love is free from nearly all forms of Personal Emotional Dependence, agape love has tremendous enduring power–it is the kind of love that never fails.

Here is a description of agape love[27]–the type of love that is free from Personal Emotional Dependence:

" Love is patient, love is kind.
It does not envy, it does not boast, it is not proud.
It is not rude, it is not self-seeking, it is not easily angered,
it keeps no record of wrongs.
Love does not delight in evil but rejoices with the truth.
It always protects, always trusts, always hopes, always perseveres.
Love never fails..."
Cor (13: 4-8)

New International Version Bible (©1978)

Putting feelings under perspective

In the attempt to understand how we can nurture a relation-ship for true love to be revealed and flourish, it is important to discuss the role of feelings as we human beings are emo-tional beings, creatures who long for passionate, awesome, thrilling excitements! Feelings of eros–feelings of infatua-tion, of romance and passion, not just for our partner, but also for all *roles* we have in life. Plato defines *eros* beyond the sphere of physical, sexual desire as "the pursuit of eros colors all aspects of our being, all of life." This is the reason we have phrases such as philanthropist (lover of humans), art lover, (lover of art), dog lover (people passionate with animals) etc.

Note that such breath-taking feelings of *wholeness*, con-tentment, and meaning could also be felt by engaging in self-destructive activities such as the use of illegal drugs, the consumption of large amounts of alcohol etc. Yet, such artificial sources of love are of short-term nature. Once their effect is finished, they leave us with emptiness and despair, because the use of such chemicals are just *desperate attempts* to satisfy the *void* of Personal Emotional Dependence (our personal *Oúhou-oúhou*). Those feelings are not long last-ing anyway–they may take us on a trip to heaven; yet, the trip is short and once finished, we are back to hell–back to hopelessness, despair, and darkness, which erode our inner peace and choke our little, inner monologue further more.

In today's popular culture, we all crave for good, thrill-ing, wholesome passionate feelings–nevertheless, good enduring feelings, the result from passionate living, require some planning and work to have a long-lasting effect. The "feel good" culture with the human tendency to demand "instant gratification" is not entirely wrong. The modern culture just got it backwards, by misplacing the context, perspective, and order of how genuine feelings are created and nurtured. Good feelings do not usually happen on a random basis. In fact, if they do come randomly, usually they do not last long. In contrast, if they come when we work on them from the right perspective *using* the right strategy–we will enjoy a stable, long-lasting relation.

Let us use the bed of roses figuratively to represent a healthy loving relationship in a couple. Such beautiful flowers, to continue to unfold, need daily watering, feeding, and weeding. In the same way, loving relationships and romance–in order to grow–need continuous work, knowledge, and skill. Awesome, romantic feelings are not the product of chance, but rather the result of *commitment* of one's whole being–body, mind, emotions, and soul–for true romantic feelings to be born and for them to be long-lasting and enduring the trials and challenges of life.

Conclusion

While in the previous chapter we have learned how various forms of Personal Emotional Dependence can disguise themselves to appear as true love, in this chapter we have defined genuine love and have described the steps to reach 'agape' love–the ultimate love. The more you learn to recognize and set aside cloudy thoughts and feelings, in which *Personal Emotional Dependence is hidden*, the higher the degree of freedom you will gain, the kind of freedom that will empower you to give your partner spontaneous, unconditional love–causing your relationship to grow and blossom like a beautiful flower.

A relationship is meant to complete each other's needs spontaneously. Nevertheless, to serve and fulfill each other's needs, *we need to be free our selves*–in our thinking, in our little, inner self-talk! And the way to become free is by amusing and setting aside cloudy thinking that comes from the void of PED (our personal *Oúhou-oúhou*). The expanded freedom and detachment *from* PED will enable us to view our relationship from the right perspective and nurture each other's emotional needs spontaneously, allowing our relation with our partner to grow and mature to reach the highest form of love– *'agape' love*–as beautiful as a wild rose!

CHAPTER 13

When the Five-Step Method Does not Seem To Work: Using the "Simplicity" Principle.

Injecting simplicity into our little, inner voice

There will be times when you think that the five-step method does not work any longer: Identifying cloudy thoughts in our inner, little speech, and naming them with the name of PED (our personal *Oúhou-oúhou*) do not bring clarity to mind. It is common that with stressors and the burdens of life–when we experience stress, frustration, over-commitment, and exhaustion–we tend to think "over our heads." Any attempt to apply the five-step method by mentally categorizing and naming *emotionally charged thoughts* does not bring any inner freedom–such negatively charged thoughts are not easily amused and set aside.

To repair the perceived agony, despair and pain, your inner monologue will engage either in the mode of the 'Loser,' the 'Hunter,' or in the mode of the 'Narcissist' drama play.

In such a state of confusion, our little, inner monologue is puzzled! In an attempt to get out of frustration, be warned that your little inner self-talk will start to think *irrationally*. In this state of mind, your self-talk will start *suggesting* silly "quick-fix" solutions–whatever it takes to *escape* the pain, the confusion, despair, and the soreness of the moment. Said differently, there will be times when your little, inner voice will become reactive and defensive–and it will prompt you to decide on anything, just to relieve the pain and despair of the moment. As a result, your little, inner self-talk will tend to suggest choices and solutions of *a reactive nature*. Such *reactive thinking*, though, what it will achieve, it will intensify the enacting one of the three principal drama scripts by *over dramatizing* your circumstances. To repair the perceived agony, despair and pain, your inner monologue will engage either in the mode of the 'Loser,' the 'Hunter,' or in the mode of the 'Narcissist' drama play.

The first remedy, every time our thinking becomes confusing and frustrating, is to avoid the temptation and *refuse to give in* and take any major decision–when our little, inner monologue is on such an emotional roller coaster. To reiterate, whenever the five-step method of this little book does not 'seem' to work, as a first step, *refuse* to take any decision that will have a long-term impact in your life–because while you are in such a confusing mental state, *such choice is unlikely to be a correct one.*

Remedy: Considering the Simplicity Principle:

The "Occam's razor" Principle
"Entities should not be multiplied unnecessarily.
William of Occam.

What is the Simplicity Principle, or the "Occam's Razor"[28] Principle?

The Simplicity Principle, or the "Occam's razor" is a principle attributed to the fourteenth century *logician* and Franciscan friar; William of Occam. The principle states that *"Entities should not be multiplied unnecessarily."*

Despite the substantial contribution of the Simplicity Principle in physics, it has applications for our daily lives as well. A more understandable, practical definition of the simplicity principle is: *"In the absence of more evidence, the simplest explanation of a problem is likely to be the correct one."* To explain it even further, when you have two equally likely solutions to a problem, <u>pick the simplest</u>–as the simplest solution is (likely) the correct.

Remember, over-dramatized, cloudy thinking distorts the view of reality from simple and obvious to complex and confusing, from descent thinking to dramatic–making otherwise simple things appear as tragic, confusing, and perplexing. Now, let us be more specific, and explain how to apply the Simplicity principle to the different areas of life.

Applying The Simplicity Principle to emotional wellness

The formula of The Simplicity Principle for our emotions is: *"The simple explanation of a bad mood is the correct one."* Said differently, unless you have adequate, strong evidence to the contrary, the <u>*simplest explanation*</u> *for not feeling well is the correct one.* In other words, when it seems that the five-step technique of this book does not work, *do not forget to consider the simplest explanation* for an uneasy little, inner monologue!

Remember as a rule, that <u>*the simplest explanation (reason)*</u> for not feeling good is (likely) the correct one.

Let's not blame us, our little, inner self-talk, for every bad mood that we experience, and let us relearn basic self-care that will make positive contribution to our physical, emotional, and spiritual well-being, improving the quality of our little, inner voice. Consider the *simplest explanation* before investigating for the cause of a bad mood (for not feeling good). If we are not feeling good, it is *simply because* we did not get enough sleep the previous night, or may be because we have neglected physical exercise, breakfast, or other basic body care!

Applying the Simplicity Principle: Relearning basic self-care for our physical self

A. The understated importance of a good night's sleep:

Sleep and mood are intimately related. Keep a regular schedule and get adequate rest. Eight hours of sleep is just a typical figure. Many people may need a little more than that. You may need nine hours to feel fully awake and mentally alert. Night sleep should start early and be *uninterrupted* for an average of eight hours to be effective. In this case, the sleep formula four plus four does not equal eight–as sleep should be *continual* without interruptions. Besides, neither does sleep time which starts from 02:00 to 11:00 a.m. equals a quality, refreshing sleep. The obvious key phrase here is that *the earlier you can go to bed, the better you will feel the next morning.* The challenge is to understand the strong relationship between good sleep and good mood–and consequently, take the steps to build new sleeping habits.

If you have difficulty going to sleep early, I would recommend some *rituals* that will help to prepare you for the end of the day. For example, I plan to go to bed not later than 11:00 p.m. I start my sleep routine at 10:00 p.m. such as taking a warm shower, putting on my pajamas, and reading a relaxing book. Generally, the aim is to take those necessary steps to *wind down your mind and body* and prepare it for a lasting, refreshing sleep. In addition, whenever you can, add to your schedule a *nap* in the middle of the day's obligations and challenges. I have found that a twenty-minute nap refreshes the mind and recharges the batteries to carry on for the rest of the day.

B. Applying the Simplicity Principle:
Rediscovering the "magical" benefits of physical exercise

Physical exercise is a powerful tool for defeating clogs in our inner monologue and bad moods in our little, inner thinking. When you exercise your body, you increase your brain's levels of serotonin and dopamine naturally, making your inner self-talk flow without dead-ends, emotional blocks, and other internal noises. The key idea is to search, experiment and find a physical exercise that is right for you.

I have discovered 'Walking' exercise, as I do not prefer the gym. I have tried several other types of exercises without much success–consequently; I have stopped doing them in a short time, simply because I did not enjoy doing them. The point I want to make here is this: Do not hesitate to *experiment* with various types of physical exercise until you find the exercise that suits you and your needs. Once you have discovered the right type for you, physical exercise will become part of you, part of your daily routine, and it will be a *positive contribution* for a smooth little inner monologue. On the other hand, following a type of exercise blindly, without experimenting enough, because it was somebody else's suggestion, is likely to make you quit exercising altogether at the first opportunity–because you and your chosen sport were just not made for each other.

C. Applying the Simplicity Principle:
Rediscovering the importance of a common-sense diet

I am not a dietitian, but after having gone through a *nervous breakdown* and after having experienced all the crippling effects of clinical depression, I took a closer look at my eating habits as healthful nutrition does have a positive *psychotropic contribution* toward emotional wellness and wholeness.

Let us start with breakfast:

Because breakfast is the most important meal of the day, by trial and error, I now combine cornflakes and oatmeal with little pieces of banana or strawberry. Eating cereals can be healthful and tasty, and an exciting contribution to your mood, as you learn to combine two or more of them. To make a long story short, cereals are excellent producers of brain energy that you will need to get through the day. The key is to find the *right combination* that will work for you—the combination of cereals that will make your breakfast tasty and exciting.

For lunch, I have developed the tendency to substitute meat with fish as fish is lighter and *a better mood enhancer* compared to meat. I recommend the basic food pyramid as it provides the brain with more energy and well-being. Furthermore, I consistently prefer lighter meals, as I have found that lighter meals translate in to lighter moods. Eating raw carrots and vegetables can be also fun as they provide instant natural energy without the highs and lows of sugar-filled chocolates and pastries.

For dinner, you may nurture the habit of avoiding big meals, as such an excessive food quantity influence *negatively* the duration and quality of sleep–and therefore will influence the way you will feel the next day. If you have to eat outside, just choose a salad such as one with feta cheese or tuna; either of them can be tasty and fulfilling without being heavy on the stomach. When I have to stay at home, I tend to avoid any type of protein, by replacing high protein foods with plenty of portions of vegetables and fruits. An oatmeal biscuit, or some honey with warm milk will satisfy your body's craving for glucose and will prepare you for a good night's sleep.

Conclusion:

When your little, inner monologue gets too confused, tired, and exhausted, consider the obvious–consider the "Simplicity" principle. The simplest explanation of a bad mood is (likely) the correct one. Basic self-care has an important impact on the way we feel and think. Therefore, do not hesitate to experiment and try new ways regarding your individual sleeping habits, physical exercise, and daily diet, until you *become conscious* what is working for you–and you will soon will be on the way for a better little, inner monologue and mood.

CHAPTER 14

When the "Five-Step" Method does not seem to work: When Tragedy Strikes

Because of our paradoxical, dramatic, human nature and the imperfect–sometimes, inhuman world in which we live– there are going to be times when we will experience a tragic loss in life. As a result, we go through deep feelings of grief and sorrow because of such great loss.

The nature of Grief

Grief is the how human emotions react to a great loss in our lives. Grief, or the way our little, inner monologue reacts to a major loss, is painful, sorrowful, and stressful– nevertheless, *grief is a normal and necessary transitory journey we must all make.* Whether it is the physical death of a loved one, the end of a loving relationship, a painful divorce, or the loss of a career, we react to the event with grief; for many people, such dreadful loss is often more frightening than death itself!

Common feelings of grief:

Whether we have lost someone or something we value so much, every one of us *reacts differently* to life's tragedies. Grief affects everyone differently. Moreover, there are some feelings of grief that are *common* to all.

Because of a sudden loss in our lives, grief kicks in with painful feelings of shock and disbelief. When we grieve, we experience feelings of unrecoverable loss, sorrow, sadness, guilt, and regret, along with intense feelings of injustice, anger, and envy–or even the emotion of anger with ourselves for what *we have not done* to avoid such an unbearable loss.

Grief and Behavior

Grief also affects behavior and the way we function as human beings. You may find it affecting you in some, or all, of the following ways:

Disturbed sleep, loss of appetite, restlessness, and exhaustion, preoccupation, anxiety, and panic attacks. You may also experience the inability to cope, *loss of interest in the little pleasures of life,* irritability, tearfulness. You may cry a lot; in fact, sometimes it is all you can do. Crying can bring relief as it is a physical outlet for the emotions, tension and strain that have built up. Other physical symptoms may include heart palpitations, nausea, dizziness, tightness in the throat and digestive problems–all of these can be felt during grieving.

(If you are concerned, consult an occupational health nurse counselor or your family doctor.)

Grief versus Clinical Depression

From the above description of the painful feelings we experience during grief, it looks as if I am describing *the symptoms of clinical depression.* I would like to emphasize, however, that <u>grief is not depression;</u> in fact, grief is *very different* from clinical depression in the following ways:

Feelings of sadness, sorrow, and depression are an integral part of grieving process–nevertheless, grief itself is not a disorder. According to *"The Diagnostic and Statistical Manual of Mental Disorders (DSM-IV),"*[29]depression-like symptoms associated with grief are considered a "normal" reaction to loss and are considered *a transitory stage*–provided they do not last too long:

1. Grief may or may not develop into clinical depression. When we learn what grief is, how to cope with it, and how to get support from doctors, friends, and significant others, depression-like symptoms of grief diminish over time, making the probability of a clinical depression less likely to occur.

2. It should be emphasized that the full spectrum of depressive symptoms may accompany the normal grieving process. Nevertheless, typically, grief does not include the *loss of self-esteem* and the enduring, overall *sense of guilt* that accompanies clinical depression.

Dr. Alan Wolfelt in *"Death and Grief: A Guide for Clergy"*[30] writes that there are several important indications and clues that *distinguish* grief from clinical depression:

1. Responsiveness to comfort and support

While the grieving individual responds to comfort and support, the person suffering from clinical depression does not.

2. Anger

Regarding *anger*, grieving people are more likely to be openly angry, although *clinically depressed individuals become unable to express their feelings*–especially to express feelings of anger in an open way.

3. Reference to the loss experienced

Although grieving people relate their depressed feelings and symptoms *specifically* to the loss they have experienced, clinically depressed individuals *do not relate them to a particular life event.*

4. Enjoyment of little pleasures of life:

Grieving people can still enjoy life's little pleasures, while individuals suffering from clinical depression exhibit an all pervading sense of doom, gloom, and a hopeless, foggy, little, inner monologue.

5. Presence of Physical complaints:

While grief is accompanied by physical complaints similar to clinical depression, *such physical effects are transitory.* In clinical depression, on the other hand, such physical symptoms *persist* over time.

6. *Expressiveness of guilt*

In addition, grieving people may express feelings of guilt regarding some particular aspects of the tragic loss they suffered. Clinically depressed persons, nevertheless, have *generalized feelings of guilt*, which have been *infused into every area in their little, inner monologue*–making people incapable of identifying and expressing such feelings.

7. *Self esteem*

Although grieving people may experience a temporary and transitory loss of self-esteem, clinically depressed persons suffer a loss of self-esteem that is enduring and colours their entire, little, inner monologue.

"The Four Tasks of Grief"[31]

Four Strategies for Surviving Tragic loss and Grief

Grief, because of a major loss in our lives, is less likely to develop into clinical depression, when we handle grief effectively and skillfully. Here are four simple steps toward surviving tragedy and great loss:

A. *Verbalize your great loss until it becomes real*

Find a practical way to speak and *express thoroughly* of what has happened–find ways to express your feelings about the great loss you have just suffered *until it becomes real to you.* Express your grieving feelings by describing to others *how* this tragic loss has affected your personal life *by verbalizing every side of it.* You can speak to a caring friend, a mental health professional, or to a support group that is related to the great loss. The key is to *speak up your feelings about your tragic loss until you do not need to tell it any longer.* By doing so, you will come closer and closer to *accept* what has happened.

B. *Express the grieving Emotions:*

Grief is filled with conflicting tidal waves of emotions. Just when you think you have accepted the death, or loss, disbelief may sweep over you again. You may feel intense anger along with equally intense feelings of love and loss. Alternatively, in the midst of crying about the person's death, a sense of unreality may surface again. No matter what the range of emotions, all are to be expected during grief. It is essential to get the emotions out of you! "Locked" feelings can build, and become overwhelming. Scream, cry, write, draw, punch a punch-bag, tell an empathetic someone, take a walk, DO SOMETHING to express what you feel.

Fully *express all your emotions* that are directly related to the loss, however contradictory or subtle they seem to be. Developing various ways of expressing your emotions until you say, "enough is enough" is so important as unexpressed emotions are depression prone! This is especially true for men, as our Western culture has taught us that we have to be 'strong' and that "men don't cry." Whether you are a man or a woman, you can use different ways to express grief such as writing your own drama play of what has happened–speak and verbalize it, let yourself cry, and talk to someone you trust and let your feelings flow.

C. Make sense of why that loss took place

Nothing can make what has happened "okay!" Life is turned upside down and changed forever. However, you can determine that something good and reasonable will come out of the unreasonable tragedy that you have just suffered. Nothing can take away the *good times* you have experienced with that person, or situation before the loss. In addition, there are *some lessons life has taught you* through the loss that can strengthen your character. On the practical level, when you are ready, you may reach out to others with similar experiences and help them in the similar loss they have experienced, or work in causes to improve the lives of others. There are ways to make meaning from tragedy and create something positive from such a dreadful loss–many charities have been founded by grieving families wanting to do more, so others do not have to suffer a similar pain.

Although nothing could restore the previous state of affairs after what has happened, get a "why"–it helps! Said differently, develop a story that would justify and explain *why this has happened to you.* Do not hesitate to involve and use the supernatural, sometimes–irrational way in explaining what has happened to you. For example, it may be that it was God's will that you do not understand now, but you will do in the end. Or, it may be better for you that such loss has happened now rather than later. Go ahead and write your story in a piece of paper. Be precise. Remember, people can endure anything, any sorrow or obstacle when they have *meaningful answers* to their question, *"why and why me?"*

D. Creating a new relationship with the great loss.

Whether the great loss has to do with the physical loss of a loved one, the loss of a romantic relationship, or any other unrecoverable loss in your life, *you can learn to create a new relationship with such loss.* No one can take away *your memories* that are connected with that person, relationship, or state of affairs. Cherishing those memories will help you realize that you have something in you that *will never die while you cherish those memories. Remembering and cherishing the memories* will allow you not to live in a shadow of the past; it is a healthful way of keeping the positive things from your past *alive* in order to give you the moral strength to carry on.

Conclusion:

There will be times when we will suddenly experience a great, unrecoverable loss in life. In the less-than-perfect world we live, a tragic loss–loss of any type–is possible. Learning the nature of grief and the main strategies how to cope with it, will help the grieving transition to be *smoother and quicker*. It should be emphasized that <u>grief is not depression</u>. Grief is just a *transitory stage* in which our emotions adjust themselves to the great loss that has just taken place. On the other hand, depression has a more permanent nature and duration. Clinical depression and the symptoms of it *endure* over time, although symptoms of grief do not shape into permanent patterns feelings and behavior when we handle it well–and suddenly life will once again take on a rosy glow like sunshine after the rain, singing a brand-new song. . . .

CHAPTER 15

Rewriting your True Life Script: Addressing the Spiritual Dimension of our Humanity

It would have been too easy for me if I was to exclude from this little book the chapter on spirituality and religion, as religion is often controversial and can bring confusion, arguments and misunderstandings among people. Psychology, anyway, is the study of the soul, the human psyche, and it is not so much interested in the spiritual and supernatural side of human nature. Then again, I would not have been true to myself, to my true life script, and honest to you, the reader, if I had excluded this chapter from the book, as the discovery of my spiritual self has led to a vast improvement in my little, inner monologue. As a result, it brought much relief to my depression–a discovery that has allowed me more access to, and realization of my true life script and inner freedom.

Why Spirituality?

The spiritual dimension of human nature is difficult to prove as it is not easily quantified and measured, so we can reach conclusions through science, using experimental and other scientific methods. Nevertheless, the existences of so many religions in the world attest the reality of humanity's spiritual needs–needs that cry out to be met, and satisfy the hunger of man's soul. The five-step method I have described in previous chapters can appeal just to your psyche (your soul), the emotional/cognitive component of human nature. Because emotions and spirits are closely interwoven, we need also to look closely and *detect and address* your spiritual needs as well.

Ignoring the spiritual dimension of human nature creates a large void in our hearts, and if we fail to fill this void in the correct way, it can create a trigger point for the enactment of the three principal drama scripts that lead to destructive habits and behaviors. We human beings are physical, emotional as well as spiritual entities–ignoring one of the three parts of the human composition, therefore, can bring imbalance and endanger the wholeness of humanity. As I have mentioned in previous chapters, human beings are mysterious, paradoxical creatures, because the vast potential for improvement is accompanied with an unfortunate gravity toward error and negativity–the inclination for self-destruction!

Diogenis of Sionope

The poor philosopher, Diogenes used to hold a night lamp, in the middle of the day, walking and searching in the streets of Athens to find . . . an honest man.

A good example that *proves* the paradox of human nature is Diogenis[32], the Greek philosopher, who was born in Sinope, Asia minor about 412 BC and lived in Athens during 423-312 B. C. Diogenes lived during the golden era of Pericles, a period that was the pinnacle of one of the greatest civilization history has ever known. There was never a period when humanity had experienced such an explosive development of the sciences such as mathematics, physics, astronomy, and medicine. During that era, the first genuine democracy was developed and flourished, not to mention an exponential growth in the arts such as classical architecture and sculpture, philosophy and the theatre with the first tragedy, the first comedy–to name just few! Even today, in many ways, we all strive to attain the unsurpassed standards and accomplishments of the ancient Greek world. The achievements of classical Athens are still admired by scholars in every field, because they have provided the foundations for today's Western civilization–as most of historians agree.

Nevertheless, the *tragedy and drama* of such an advance civilization was exposed by Diogenes, a contemporary citizen of classical Athens: The poor philosopher, Diogenes[33] used to hold a night lamp, in the middle of the day, walking and searching in the streets of Athens to find . . . an honest man! Disappointed by the serious character flaws in human nature such as dishonesty, arrogance and greed, in the midst of one of the greatest civilizations ever developed, Diogenes *believed* civilization to be regressive and not a progressive development of human nature, because civilization has contributed little to the real advancement of the human spirit and character.

The Abyss of the Human Heart

Even in the Greek culture of today, we speak of the human psyche to be an abyss! *"An abyss is the soul of man,"*[34] we whisper, every time we are confronted with news of the conduct of otherwise peaceful, ordinary people, who suddenly commit serious crimes–atrocities that spring from the human inclination toward error–the irony, paradox and contradiction of human nature. The abyss in our soul becomes evident in the three principal drama scripts we enact daily, manifesting the huge void in our hearts and spirits–the abyss that is no other than the vacuum of our Personal Emotional Dependence (the void created by our personal *Oúhou-oúhou*).

Sharing similar feelings with Diogenes, we may seriously question why we boast so much about today's technological advances, when human relations are so swallow, poor, short-term, and transitory. If there was a better way that we could possibly define civilization, it would be how an advancement in any field had resulted in an improvement in the contact between human beings. I wonder sometimes, how we can enjoy the advances of technology when we do not have genuine friends to share them with–when the interactions and relations with other human beings are so egotistic, individualistic, passive, impersonal, and numb....

Despite the technological achievements of modern man, with our high-tech laptops and the "state of the art" cellular phones, Mother Teresa shared a similar opinion. In a journey made by Mother Teresa to the United States of America, and to other Western countries, she described the loneliness that exists in the affluent, Western world as a *plague* much worst than the typhus and leprosy that she has seen, or has treated in the developing nations, where she served. No wonder the incidents of depression are lower in developing, agricultural nations, and much higher in developed, post-modern societies. Although we can cure physical diseases with modern surgery and medicine, we just cannot cure hopelessness, despair, and loneliness that trouble people in modern societies.

"There are many in the world who are dying for a piece of bread, but there are many more dying for a little love."[35]
Mother Teresa.

Searching for a "Redeemer"

Because of the serious character flaws in human nature, it is becoming noticeable that no amount of philosophy, medicine, or science can correct the human paradox, our human condition–the abyss in our human heart. Consequently, the need for a "Redeemer" becomes exceptionally obvious.

A Cry Out for Redemption:
"Euripedes's The deus ex machina."[36]

Somehow, the first tragedian subconsciously
realized that humanity has been running on empty–
operating on the "tragedy mode" –running aimlessly
on a tragic, catastrophic drama script.

The Greek tragedian Euripides is often criticized for his frequent use of the "Deus Ex Machina," when things get so difficult and dramatic that the gods *intervene and solve directly* an unsolvable, tragic situation—a tragic set of circumstances, human beings just could not figure out. Somehow, the first tragedian subconsciously realized that humanity has been running on empty–operating on the "tragedy mode" –running aimlessly on a tragic, catastrophic drama script and the gods have to *intervene and heal human tragedies*. Indeed, more than half of Euripides's tragedies use a "deus ex machine" in their resolution–implying humanity's apparent failure to remedy human issues, perplexities, and challenges that come from our paradoxical, contradictory, human nature.

Today more than ever, the thirst for divine redemption is manifested in several ways such as the hunger for money, power and control, the excessive use of alcohol or sex–anything that will temporarily *fill the void* in the human heart–*the void that only God can fill!* As human beings wonder aimlessly through life, they learn in the end that these "fixes" are not enduring–they do not set people free—such fixes just sink people further in to their devouring Personal Emotional Dependence, and the enslaving drama scripts they so passionately enact.

Humanity's great need for a Redeemer

If we cannot fix ourselves from our propensity toward error with the use of science, political systems, various philosophies, and technological advancements, then the creator of the universe–He who has created us first is the one who can heal us and *re-create us* again. With His redemptive power of the cross, He can be the only one who can set us free from our propensity toward error and vice. The human race, humanity's dramatic nature, our potential for good and evil, the erroneous DNA of the human psyche and false heart–can be redeemed and renewed just by the creator Himself! The supernatural, redemptive power of God can change your human nature by giving you *a new heart*, creating in you a new sense of freedom, zeal, bringing you the true meaning of life.

Knowing God the right way:

Developing a Personal Relationship with your Creator

If the creator cares and governs the universe with such a flawless, mathematical accuracy, how much more He will be interested to rectify you as He cares for you–because you are more valuable to Him than cosmos.

The ruler of the universe has created you in the first place, and He is the one who can re-create you again–if you *search* for Him with all your heart—if you are willing to trust Him and begin a personal relationship with Him. It is a scientific fact that your brain, even when in error, is far more complex and mysterious than the stars of the universe. Therefore, a single human being *like you* is more valuable to God than cosmos with all the galaxies, planets, and stars in it. It is not a surprise to know that scientists know more about outer space than the space between our ears–the mystery of the human mind. If the creator cares and governs the universe with such a flawless, mathematical accuracy, how much more He will be interested to rectify you as He cares for you–*because you are more valuable to Him than cosmos!*

You and God have unfinished business–you have open accounts to settle! For some unknown, mysterious reasons, you matter to Him.

You and God, face to face

You and God have unfinished business–you have open accounts to settle! For some unknown, mysterious reasons, *you matter to Him!* As He is a gentle being, He respects your precious freedom–therefore, He will not force Himself on you unless you make the first step. The creator of the universe is knocking at the door of your life waiting for you to open. He is not willing to force His will on you as He values your freedom. He respects your choice to either ignore Him or accept Him–in the house of your being–in your precious heart.

If you could just trust Him. If you could allow Him to enter in the core of your soul, He will rectify your erroneous little, inner monologue–He will liberate you from the enslaving power of your Personal Emotional Dependence, setting you free from your personal *Oúhou-oúhou*. God can bring simplicity and harmony in your self-talk as you have never experienced or thought was possible.

My Story, My witness:

Depression, hopelessness, suffering, and its accompanying negative emotions (fear, frustration, and despair) have brought me to the feet of God. He has taught me that I am neither alone nor helpless. My personal relationship with Him reminds me daily that that *I matter to Him*, and that my life is not merely a biological, random event in a *chaotic, meaningless* universe.

> *If I could tell you! If I could convey with words how much my little, inner monologue has been improved! I wish, if I could find the right words to describe how every molecule of my being was changed and transformed by Him–through His redemptive power and sweet fellowship with His spirit.*

Before my first contact with God, I never knew that the creator of the cosmos was interested in me personally, intimately–face to face–heart to heart! In fact, however many attempts I have made to reach and fill the void deep in my Personal Emotional Dependence, nothing compared with the intimacy I have experienced with the creator of the universe in a warm, personal, intimate way.

If I could tell you! If I could convey with words how much my little, inner monologue has been improved! I wish, if I could find the right words to describe how every molecule of my being was changed and transformed by Him–through His redemptive power of the cross and sweet fellowship with His spirit.

You are not alone!

Despite your life's drama, however wrong and tragic it might have been, let me assure you are a sacred being! You are a rare human being–the crown of creation as it is implied in the Holy Scriptures. For some inexplicable reasons, *you matter to Him!* With God, you have a purpose and a future–in fact, God is not finished with you until your last breath! If you are willing to give up your false, volatile, chaotic drama script and follow God seriously, He will put you on the right path, in the right life script, and give you such freedom, enduring peace, and empowerment–such augmented faith, that you can literally walk through the burning coals of life without getting burned.

The deeper you are willing to get to know Him, the more freedom you will experience over your enslaving drama script, your foggy little, inner monologue, and you will eventually *triumph* over your adverse circumstances and challenges of life. By choosing Him over the 'things' of this world, He will put you in to a new life script in which you will be free from the circumstances of life, setting you free indeed! God is whispering to you right now:

> *"I alone know the plans I have for you,*
> *plans to bring you prosperity and not disaster,*
> *plans to bring about the future you hope for.*

Then you will call to me.
You will come and pray to me,
and I will answer you.
You will seek me, and you will find me
because you will seek me with all your heart."

Jeremiah 29:11-13 Good News Bible ©

Distinguishing Religion from true Spirituality: Three drama scripts Religious people fall into.

True spirituality is a spontaneous, personal relationship you enjoy with the creator of the universe, by gradually allowing His redemptive power to change and empower you from the inside out–by constantly filling the void in your Personal Emotional Dependence with grace, love and forgiveness. On the other hand, religion, any religion for that matter– (whether we talk about religions of totalitarian regimes or the religion of Christian fundamentalism of developed nations)–is the human attempt to change others, systems, society, philosophy, politics, from the outside-in approach–<u>on the excuse of good intentions</u>! Religion *will enslave you back to the three principal drama scripts,* while a genuine, personal relationship with your creator will *set you free,* allowing you to live your true life script.

Religion versus genuine Spirituality
Religion will enslave you back to the three principal drama scripts, while a genuine, spontaneous, intimate relationship with your Creator will set you free, allowing you to live your true life script.

Through my quest for genuine spirituality, I have encountered three ways in which believers have turned back to their old, enslaving drama scripts:

160

A. The 'Loser' Religious drama script

In my walk with God, I have seen genuine believers turning bitter, having been infected by a strange, poisonous belief that God owes them something. They think God is there to meet their every desire, while He just promised to meet the needs of their heart! They engage in this "Loser" miserable drama script, blaming God for every misfortune that occurs in their life. Demanding paradise here and now, they somehow forget that God promised them a *saving ship*, a peaceful, joyful heart in the midst of difficulties–not a luxurious "love" boat.

A healthy relationship with the creator of the universe does not depend on life's troubles and adverse circumstances. On the contrary, God promised to be with you and give you the strength and the peace that is needed to go *through* the tragic circumstances of your life, shaping and strengthening in this way your character and preparing you for heaven–our real home!

B. The Religious 'Hunter' Drama Script

Such religious groups have an implied slogan,
"religion by works, not just by the grace of God."

Because of the abundant freedom and unconditional love they have experienced during their first contact with God, such persons have mistakenly substituted God with their utopian, Personal Emotional Dependence (their personal *Oúhou-oúhou*). In this unhealthy relationship, God and their Personal Emotional Dependence (their personal *Oúhou-oúhou*) become one and the same. In response to this confusion in their little, inner self-talk, they fall back to their old 'Hunter' drama script by endlessly attempting to reach and please God by good works. Such religious groups have an implied slogan, "religion by works, not just by the *grace* of God." They continually 'do' things for God to reach His infinite grace, ignoring the fact that the grace of God already rests in their heart. This type of overzealous, religious groups are never satisfied, as they seem to forget how to 'be' with God and 'rest' intimately in Him and in His enduring peace.

C. The 'Self-righteous' Religious drama script

The self-righteous legalistic drama script represents religious people who think God has assigned them a mission to change the world, when in reality God is interested *in changing them first*. This type of believers with "the end justifies the means" conviction, ignore the fact that God changes people, effecting change *in the heart, from the inside out* and not from the outside in. The self-righteous, Narcissistic religious drama script is subtle and can be very dangerous, as many religious and political leaders take advantage of people's sincere faith in God to serve *their purposes* and agendas.

I wonder how many wars and crimes have been committed against humanity when believers got into and still get into this deceptive, self-righteous, conceited drama script, in which they believe they can change the world–while Jesus warned them that real change must come from within their heart–when they allow Him to change them first.

ᏣᎤ

Freedom and the true Believer

As I said, there is still another group of believers, though a small one. This group follow God's heart and His directions *patiently* without complaining, reacting, and fussing. You can see the evidence of God's grace from the smile on their glowing faces that they obediently follow God and *enjoy* His close presence. Their intimacy with God continue to grow through the years *despite* what life throws at them. Their inner freedom to love and follow God is astonishing. The truly free believer realizes that God is his genuine father; nevertheless, the believer does not behave like a spoiled child–the believer realizes that his relationship with God is a "work in process" in this tragic world we live. They know that God is not a magician. Although He sometimes works through miracles, many times He works *quietly in the background*, turning every bad thing to our good, in good times as well as in bad times.

This small group of believers are free from their Personal Emotional Dependence (their personal *Oúhou-oúhou*), as they preserve their inner freedom and wait patiently for Him, even when they feel He is not there for them–usually at times when they need Him the most. Through the *intimate relationship* with their creator, they maintain their inner peace, shining grace, and smile, even when a prayer for a great need seems to go unnoticed by Him. These believers continue to enjoy *close contact* with God who in turn nourishes and expands their *inner freedom* and empowers them to triumph over the hardships of life. They refuse to give in to the temptation that will enslave them back in their false drama scripts, and they continue regardless, even when their physical and mental pain seems too much to bear. Oh! how truly free are they–they are free indeed!

> *"Even though the fig trees have no fruit and*
> *no grapes grow on the vines,*
> *even though the olive crop fails and the fields*
> *produce no grain,*
> *even though the sheep all die and the cattle*
> *stalls are empty,*
> *I will still be joyful and glad, because the LORD*
> *God is my saviour.*
> *The Sovereign LORD gives me strength.*
> *He makes me sure-footed as a deer*
> *and keeps me safe on the mountains."*

Habbaku 3:17-19. Good News Bible © 1992

Conclusion:

Discovering the spiritual side of your human nature can be a catalyst in satisfying your deepest needs, fulfilling the spiritual hole and void in your personal Emotional dependence (your personal *Oúhou-oúhou*). Religion *will enslave you back to three principal drama scripts,* while a genuine, *intimate relationship* with your creator will *set you free,* allowing you to live your true life script, living a life with freedom, purpose, hope, and meaning.

Epilogue

You have finished this book. What have you read? Simply a series of principles and a simple, workable technique for altering your little, inner monologue–a simple, five-step method that *amuses and sets aside* depressive and cloudy thoughts. With these tools, inner freedom is now attainable; it is within your reach. You have learned a new-old set of principles, which have recreated the essence of your human nature. You have also learned a workable formula to put the concepts and techniques into practice.

Nevertheless, reading the concepts and formula once is not enough. Please go back and persistently practice the new formula and concepts you have learned. Do not worry about the effort it takes to internalize them–adverse circumstances are usually the best teachers. Just consistently go back, review the concepts, the formula, and redo the exercises of the book. Keep reviewing the concepts and the techniques until you obtain the desired results, until you reach the desired freedom from depressive thoughts.

I wrote this book out of a sincere desire to help you. I have absolute confidence and belief in the principles and methods of this book as they have been tested in the reality of life's adverse circumstances by many people–including myself. The formula and concepts of the book work when worked. They will bring immense inner freedom to your thinking the more you learn to use them in your little, inner self-talk and apply them to everyday living.

It will be great happiness to know that this small book has helped you to *de-dramatize* your life and defeat clinical depression. We may have never met in person, but in this book, we have met as we have shared the same struggle, the same agony and despair in battling depression. Through this little book, we have become spiritual friends. I pray for you that God will help you–so believe and live a life with a new sense of freedom, a new meaning, and a new perspective.

The author

snicolaou2011@gmail.com

Bibliography

[1] Adler, Alfred. (1956). *The Individual Psychology of Alfred Adler*. (New York: Harper Torchbooks.)

[2] Epictetus, *The Manual of Epictetus*, translated into English by James Sandford, 1567

[3] Braiker, H.B. (1989). *"The Power of Self-Talk."* Psychology Today, December, pp. 23-27

[4] Epictetus, *The Manual of Epictetus*, translated into English by James Sandford, 1567

[5] Buie, J. (1988). *'Me' decades generate depression: individualism erodes commitment to others.* APA Monitor, 19(18)

[6] *"Handbook of Epictetus"* trans. Nicholas P. White, Hackett Publishing Company, 1983, (Chapter five of the handbook)

[7] Robert Collier quotes (American motivational author, 1885-1950).

[8] Thomas Bulfinch "Bulfinch's Mythology - Burkert 1985, p. 198.

[9] Plato, *"Sophist"* ,written 360 B.C.E

[10] G.B. Kerferd, *"The Sophistic Movement"* Cambridge University Press (Sep 30, 1981), p. 8

[11] Maurice E. Wagner, *The Sensation of Being Somebody*, (Zondervan Publishing Company, 1985), p192

[12] *"And in Man is a three-pound brain which, as far as we know, is the most complex and orderly arrangement of matter in the universe."* Isaac Asimov, *"In the Game of Energy and Thermodynamics You Can't Even Break Even,"* Smithsonian, August 1970, p. 10.

[13] *"I will praise thee; for I am fearfully and wonderfully made…"* King James Bible, Psalms 139:14

[14] Victor E. Frankl, *Man's Search For Meaning* (New York: Washington Square, Press Pocket Books, 1984), p.85

[15] 12 Black, Robert, Morris, Saul, & Jennifer Bryce. *"Where and Why Are 10 Million Children Dying Every Year?"* The Lancet 361:2226-2234. 2003.

[16] *"Smile at life, and life will smile back at you"* - Traditional Greek-Cypriot quote, cited by Chrystalla Theodorou Nicolaou.

[17] Victor E. Frankl, *Man's Search For Meaning* (New York: Washington Square, Press Pocket Books, 1984), p.172

[18] Thomas Harris, *I'm OK-You're OK* (Avon; First Edition, 1976), p 49.

[19] *"Tantalus." Encyclopedia Mythica* from Encyclopedia Mythica Online.
<http://www.pantheon.org/articles/t/tantalus.html>
[Accessed December 03, 2009].

[20] *"Narcissus."* Encyclopedia Mythica from Encyclopedia Mythica Online.
<http://www.pantheon.org/articles/n/narcissus.html>
[Accessed December 03, 2009].

[21] Quote by Michael Novak, author of *"Business as a Calling."*

[22] Commencement address at Stanford University by Steve Jobs, on June 12, 2005

[23] C.P Cavafy - The official website of the Cavafy Archive

[24] Ithaca by C.P Cavafy. From *"The Poems 1897-1933"*, Ίκαρος Publishing 1984

[25] Plato, *Phaedrus* 249E: *"He who loves the beautiful is called a lover because he partakes of it"*

[26] Aristotle, *"things that cause friendship are: doing kindnesses; doing them unasked; and not proclaiming the fact when they are done"* (Rhetoric, II. 4, trans. Rhys Roberts).

[27] *Agape love: 1Cor (13: 4-8) New International Version Bible (©1984)*

[28] Occam's Razor Principle: *"Entities should not be multiplied unnecessarily."* Merriam-Webster's Collegiate Dictionary (11th ed.). New York: Merriam-Webster. 2003. ISBN 0-87779-809-5. http://www.merriamwebster.com/dictionary/Occam%27s%20razor.

[29] American Psychiatric Association. , *"Diagnostic and statistical manual of mental disorders."* 4th ed. Washington, D.C.1994

[30] Dr. Alan Wolfelt, *"Death and Grief: A Guide for Clergy."*

[31] *"The Four Tasks of Grief"* - Distributed by The Link Counseling Center's National Resource Center for Suicide Prevention and Aftercare, 348 Mt. Vernon Highway, N.E., Atlanta, GA 30328

[32] *"Lives and Opinions of Eminent Philosophers"* Laërtius (vi. 76)

[33] *"Lives and Opinions of Eminent Philosophers"* Laërtius (vi. 41)

[34] *"Abyss is the soul of man."* Traditional Greek quote.

[35] *"We can cure physical diseases with medicine, but the only cure for loneliness, despair, and hopelessness is love. There are many in the world who are dying for a piece of bread, but there are many more dying for a little love"* Author - Mother Teresa

[36] "Deus ex machine" Rehm (1992, 72) and Walton (1984, 51).